YESTERDAY'S IRELAND

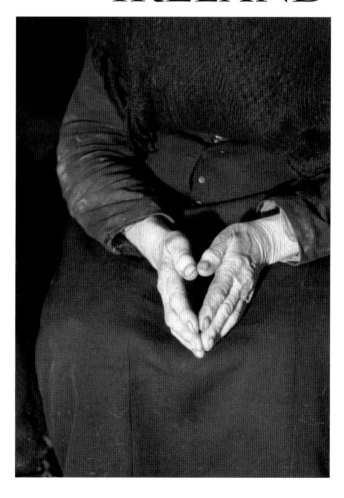

Paddy Linehan

YESTERDAY'S IRELAND

David & Charles

Contents

To Angela and Kevin Treacy
for being good

Sitting in the Hob

'Long ago, in houses throughout rural Ireland sitting in the hob was a position to be coveted. And as a child growing up in Ireland there was nothing I loved more than sitting in the hob in my grandmother's house listening to stories. The hob was the little stone seat, part of the fireplace itself, way in out of the cold and tucked so far back that, if you looked up, you could see the night sky through the chimney opening. If you were sitting in the hob when it rained you might even catch the odd drop on the head, if there was no wind and the rain was coming straight down.'

Strong enough to pull a
plough ... or fight the fight.

S itting in the hob was heaven on earth. In most cases it was reserved for the old lady or man of the house, but little boys, if they were very good, got to sit there for a 'spelleeen' (short while) before they went off 'up them stairs to bed'. I laboured against the odds at being good; the reward was well worth it.

I sat there enthralled. Every night I filled anew with wonder and awe that fuelled an inner glow of happiness. I thought the old men sitting around telling the stories were vessels of wisdom and knowledge. I never asked any questions because I believed the chasm between them and me was too great to be bridged by any words of mine. I was afraid, too, that I would sound stupid. The world they talked about was way above the one I occupied; questions or comments from a 'little boy' would be at least presumptuous, maybe even cheeky. And cheeky would definitely bar one from the hob for life.

Though they talked about olden times – 'the good ol' days' – I thought they themselves were always old. My young mind hadn't yet grasped the reality of passing time. I thought my childhood would last forever; I thought the talkers were always the age they were now, and that time wasn't marching on but standing still. We were stuck in the dull present. We would never again witness the wonders they had.

I listened to fantastic stories of feats of strength and endurance; of men so strong they pulled ploughs; of fights at fairs and matches so ferocious that only a fraction of those who went out came home alive. They talked of ghosts and omens, of religion, of the power of saints and the danger of 'going against the will of God', stories that came out of the very earth of Ireland.

I envied them for what they'd witnessed: they'd seen it all. Internally I cursed my misfortune for being a latecomer to this world. Why did I have to arrive after the place was already tamed? Was there nothing left for me to do to mark myself a hero? Despite what they said about 'the will of God' I thought he had made a mistake

A typical country house but there is something special about this one. The good cups and saucers are out, there is an oilcloth on the table, the children are all sitting the way they have been told to, even the granny is on best behaviour – we have a visitor.

in not sending me down a lot earlier, when there was still some things left to be done.

Overcome by turf heat, sleep and romance, I often drifted off before the stories were all told. Then someone would take me up the stairs and tuck me in. There, in dreamy fantasy on a feather bed, I filled in the ending for myself.

And maybe my fantastic endings might have been as real as the stories themselves. They must have been embellished. Maybe the good men didn't intend to do that, but it's only human nature – we look at the past through a nicely tinted magnifying glass. That's the way we are, and a good thing that is, too. We romanticize; we remember all the summers of our youth as endless days of sunshine and flowers, of birdsong and laughter. It must have rained, but do we remember it?

In my youth, in the 1940s and 1950s, it was customary for families to visit their grandparents quite often. Mine lived in a place of small farms, on the border between Cork and Kerry, near a little village called Knocknagree. Recently I returned from abroad and heard the old place was passed on. I was told an ambitious young man now owned the house and that he had great plans for it. I decided to go and have a look.

There was a new iron gate now, with lock and chain, so I didn't use that way in. I went round the side instead. The old *boreen* (a little road) up the back was still the same. The ferns were still beside the stream and the lady's fingers – foxgloves – too. My mother loved to pick them. The blackthorn was there. She wouldn't touch that: bad luck followed the blackthorn. It was bigger and more angry looking. More gnarled, too; it looked down on my advance with as much menace as it ever had. I even recognized the stones – many of them still

A good finish to a rick of turf not only looked good, the rain ran off it like water off a duck's back.

There is a swish of business to this man with his bicycle by the head. He could be coming home with important news – or maybe with a few drinks in his belly. Cottages like the one on the left would now be a tourist attraction – so would the man with the bike.

in the same spot as before, and the elevated stone platform at the corner of the house where we kept the milk churns. I half expected Rose, the sheepdog, to come barking round the corner at me, but she wasn't there; nor were the geese and turkeys.

The rick of turf was gone.

No need now for that; there was a green plastic tank where it used to stand, more erect than the rick ever was, but hardly as attractive.

Once there were carts in an open shed beside the rick.

Surprise!

They were still there. Nearly exactly as they were, but not for use. Now they're for display, 'relics of past times'. Their metal bits were blackened and the wood painted brighter than it ever was before. But the same carts – no doubting that; I recognized the pattern of the splinters on the shafts. The old people would use these carts for taking the churns of milk to the creamery after milking the cows.

Sometimes they allowed the children to sit on the shafts and travel with them. I remember making pictures of the patterns of wear and splintering. I see them again now – the same splinters. The old pictures come to mind. As we rattled down the stony *boreen* the pictures moved around and we tried our best to stop them. Now they are still forever. The carts have come to final rest.

All *boreens* are stony. Roads are smoother. Travelling down the *boreen* you couldn't stand up because of the shaking, but once on the road you could. They weren't tarred but traffic – animal and human – had smoothed them down.

Now, on my nostalgic return visit of inspection, I travelled smoothly, too. I came by car – a fairly slick and steady Toyota from Japan. I parked it near the carts. They weren't in awe; they had seen it all before.

Long ago.

Roads were often long and dreary looking but there was always a mountain somewhere to distract you. This one is Benbo Mountain in Co. Leitrim.

I am sure if they could speak they'd tell this oriental machine a thing or two about cars. About the good ol' days when cars were tough and black and came from Fords of Cork. They'd tell this new Toyota with its electric windows and metallic finish about the fine machine they saw 'way back in '49'.

In those days my father and mother lived about sixty miles from the granny's. We usually came by train. Then, in 1949, just when we were dreaming up our summer trip, our father arrived home in a Baby Ford. He told us he had paid £24 for it in a garage near Lismore in County Waterford. 'No more train for us,' he said. 'We're off to Knocknagree by car.'

He drove at a steady speed of thirty miles an hour on the straight bits. He had to slow down a lot for the bends and pull over to let the

Humpbacked bridges and cottages by the wayside gave character to a road. They were also good landmarks for giving direction: 'A small bit over the bridge and round the bend, shure it is no distance at all if you hurry.' This is at Inishcarra in Co. Cork.

OPPOSITE:
Cars were tough and black and came from Fords of Cork. This one is climbing Patrick's Hill in Cork in 1932.

horse and carts pass. We felt good when those people looked at us, for we knew we were objects of envy. Inside the car we played with the window handles, rubbed the leather and marvelled at the smoothness of the ride. When we got there, my father parked the Baby Ford where I now parked my Toyota more than fifty years later.

Back then, the granny got an awful shock. Six of us, all arms and legs, tumbled in around the house to her. She was baking bread; her hands were full of flour. She went outside to see 'what brought ye'. There it was. She rubbed back wisps of hair to see it was not a dream. I am not sure it was only the flour that turned her white. Whether 'twas or not she couldn't wait to get rid of us – unlike her, because she was usually full of hospitality. We often stayed for days, even weeks. But this time she 'rattled up the dinner' real fast so 'ye can be on yer way'. We told her there was no hurry; all six of us told her: 'Granny, we're staying …' 'Granny, can I sleep with you …' 'No! I'm sleeping in …' 'Can I collect the eggs …' 'Granny, you promised …'

After dinner our father went to the village. He said he was going for a few pints. I am sure he was: he liked a drink and there was no law then to say a man couldn't drink and drive, but we all knew he wanted to show off the car, too. Once he had gone, our granny's reason for wanting to send us on our way revealed itself.

He wasn't home by nightfall. Granny wrung her hands. She looked at the big-faced clock. It ticked back at her: no sympathy there. She looked up at the statue of the Sacred Heart, and muttered something. My mother said, 'He'll be all right.'

'How could he be all right! How could he drive a car in the dark?'

Now, more than half a century on, the door opens, too. The new owner is 'doing the place up for the tourist'. He'll let it out for the summer months. They come from all over to rent 'old places' around here but you'd have to do it up, 'Oh! Jaysus yes! You'd have to do the ol' place up like … with the ol' central heating and all that craic … don't you know?'

I do indeed.

The owner takes me inside. The ceiling is the same, with the hooks for hanging bacon painted over. The floor has just been covered with

An experienced hand. Country homes often had built-in grannies. They were good for minding the children while the younger, stronger women did the important work on the farm. They used to say: ''tis the place outside that keeps the place inside.'

Mechanization!
Down with the handle and
up jumps the water. Will
wonders never cease?

shiny tiles. Wires snake around the walls and in and out of remembered crevices, half-concealed and half-revealed. The fire is gone. In its place a stove 'to keep the ol' character in the place, don't you see? Oh! Shure you'd have to have it authentic … they want it to be like it always was, you know?

I know.

He asks me if I'd have a cup of tea. Shure I would, I'd love a cup of tea.

He boils a plastic jug, puts a bag in a cup and I get 'tea'. I sit by the 'authentic stove', as far in as I can get. No chimney? 'Oh! No, all blocked up to stop the draught, don't you know.' You don't need a chimney when your burning oil from the Arab Gulf, chimneys are only for turf and logs and other times.

He has a son, 'a mighty man' all of five years old with baseball cap and Man Utd jersey. He sidles up and asks, 'Who are you?'

The wheel has turned; my hour has come.

'Way back in the good ol' days, long before you were born … even before your father here was born …' I'm only just in my stride telling him how great men were, how strong and brave and fearless, when he starts to yawn. The father says he's tired, that he's had a heavy day.

'Haven't you the heavy day helping Daddy? Yes indeed, we need a little rest!'

He lays him on a couch to sleep. A couch of tweed, 'to keep the thing authentic'.

This authentic 'developer' wishes me 'God speed'; he tells me it was very interesting and wishes me 'good luck and call again'.

The dusk has come. I turn on the lights but I think there is no need. I 'could drive that car in the dark'. Down this *boreen* I could anyway, because the holes and stones are where they always were, the bushes that make ghosts against the inking sky, the mountains in the distance. I wonder if the 'mighty man' on the tweed couch is dreaming in the end of my story.

Some things have changed: the turf is gone, as are the donkey and the goose. I suppose the feather bed is now foam or sprung, but the bedstead is still iron, no doubt, 'to keep the thing authentic'. But have the people changed? I don't know. Oscar Wilde said 'People don't change, only things like hats and fashions change'. I hope he was right.

Back on the road now, it is even smoother than before. There would be no problem standing up on an open cart on this road now, if one was young enough. But would I want to?

I wouldn't. But I want to tell the story. To say it like it was. The way I remember it. To talk about it as if those were better times. In truth I think they were, yet I wouldn't go back. That's a dichotomy I haven't figured out, a paradox that beats explanation. That's the way it is. And I am sure that's the way it always was.

This is no wayside cottage but a substantial farmer's house. You'd know by the strut of the geese that even they know they are a cut above the common.

CHAPTER ONE

'Around the House and Mind the Dresser…'

'On Christmas night the lighted candle was placed in the window so that if anyone was wandering the road without a place to stay for the night they would be guided by the candle. The idea came from Mary and Joseph looking for a place to stay on the first Christmas Night, but Santa used it, too, to find his way from house to house.'

I never met my great-grand mother but I knew her well. My mother lived with her from the time she was eight years old until she married my father at the age of twenty-three. She talked an awful lot about the old lady, so that is how I got to know her. I can't say exactly when great-grand mother would have been born but I estimate it to have been around the end of the Great Famine, in 1849. The most likely date is 1850. I feel I have known Ireland for a very long time. I was born in 1943 but, through my mother, her mother and grandmother, I think I have known it for a lot longer than my own lifetime.

Because of emigration almost everyone in Ireland has relations in America. These relations were very important. Young people who wanted to emigrate needed an aunt or uncle over there to claim them, otherwise they could not go. The American relations were also a source of hope for the very poor. In fifties Ireland emigrant remittances were still an item in the government figures; they helped to balance the books in an economy that had little foreign trade. And the American relations often sent clothes.

Like so many families in Ireland, ours had many such relations: the best of them was a grand aunt who had emigrated to America just before the end of the nineteenth century. I only became acquainted with her in the US – she lived in New York – in the sixties. She told me a lot about the Ireland she had left at the turn of the century. She was a lovely old lady with a heart of gold. When we were young she used to send parcels of clothes to us. They were very important: without the 'clothes from America' we would have had very little to wear. We weren't unusually poor, but in forties and fifties Ireland there weren't too many boutiques or 'designer' shops; even if they had existed there wouldn't have been a whole lot of call on them since nobody had any money to spend. Bought clothes were rare; the women made most of what was worn: they knitted socks and sweaters and made shirts, trousers and dresses.

The clothes from America were 'shop-made' and we loved them. Aunt Jua – that was the grand aunt's name – sent a few parcels of these clothes every year. When they arrived there would be a great

There was great joy in new clothes. Few could afford it so they sorted out the best they could from second hand stuff as here in Cumberland Street in Dublin.

Travelling families were big and extended and not too fussy about fashion. A good horse was central to the enterprise of constantly moving from one place to another.

scramble to open them. We'd all be in there together, all six of us, tugging at the cord and string and pulling things out, 'Oh! Look, that would fit me', 'No it wouldn't, it's too small for you, 'tis my size.' The excitement was great.

All these ladies in my life had their own view of the past, but they had one thing in common: they all thought the generation before their own had things an awful lot harder than they themselves had. I remember my mother saying things like, 'We weren't too badly off at all; we had plenty to eat anyway, but in my Ma's time they were pure slaves, and they were hungry half the time.' Though I never heard it, I am convinced that her mother and her grandmother would have said the same thing. Now I think the generation before mine were the ones that had it awful hard.

My contemporaries and I have seen more change in the last sixty years than our mothers, grandmothers, great grandmothers and any grand aunt in America put together. I think each of them had it awful hard. They didn't complain about it; actually, they mostly made it sound like things were very happy in their young days. Nostalgia about the 'good ol' days' always existed, and it always will. Though,

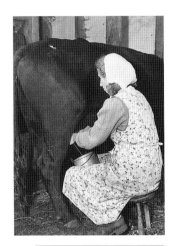

Cows were hand milked into a can held between the knees. The tune produced varied in pitch as the can filled. Those used to it didn't have to look at what they were at at all; they milked away by ear.

one autumn evening in 1967, when Jua and I were sitting in her Bronx apartment talking about old times, she said one simple little thing that revealed a lot of thinking that went on under her placid veneer. She had been in America more than seventy years at that stage and had never once been back to Ireland. She was already ninety by then. 'Aunt Jua, wouldn't you ever think of going home?' I asked her. She wagged her head in a 'no' and she said slowly, 'To tell you the truth, when I look back I see red.' She wasn't talking about danger; I think she was thinking about the hard life and maybe even hunger.

There wasn't an awful lot of change in rural Ireland from the 1850s until the 1950s. That's an understatement. The real turning point in Irish life came in the late fifties and early sixties. Up until that time the idea was that Ireland should be self-sufficient. Perhaps economic science had not developed to the point where the benefits of international trade were appreciated. This was, to some extent, the case all over, but the Irish were particularly partial to the idea. After hundreds of years of occupation, people were anxious to go it alone. They weren't anxious to be dependent on other countries for the goods and services they required.

Sean Lemass (1899–1971) changed all that. He became Taoiseach (Prime Minister) in 1959, succeeding Eamon de Valera. Intelligent and educated (a volunteer in the Easter Rising of 1916, he had escaped execution because of his youth and relatively low rank), Lemass also had foresight. He knew Ireland could not develop on a self-sufficiency policy; he knew the importance of industrialization and foreign trade. The emphasis thus moved away from farming: factories were built and jobs created. For many Irish, this movement away from rural life, centred on farming, marked the biggest change of all in their way of life.

*

Everyone who grew up in rural Ireland has their own recollections of life, of how things were from day to day. I have my own memories of Irish rural life, but some things do go back before my time. I will not interrupt the flow of the telling by differentiating between my own recollections and what they, my foremothers, told me.

*

Every house had a kitchen, of course, and every kitchen had an open fire. The fire, fuelled by turf, was the focal point of life. It boiled pots and heated the stone for the shuttle iron; it provided what heat there was for the whole house, and at night everyone sat around the fire. Over the fire was a crane, pivoted into the ground at the bottom and to a stone in the fireplace above, so that it opened in and out like a gate, one that was always black with soot. When someone wanted to take a pot off or put another one on they swung out the crane and all that was hanging on it came with it. There was always at least one pot simmering away on the crane all day, often more. There would be a pot of water anyway, and probably one of feed for the farmyard animals – hens, ducks, turkeys, geese and pigs all had to be looked after. There might be a pot of soup for the family, too.

Radios were rare and not so finely tuned. There was a lot of scraping and scratching as the wet and dry batteries ran low. You could easily be let down in the middle of a match.

These pots varied in size and shape. There were big three-legged ones for the water and animal feed, and smaller ones for lesser operations. There was a saying in Ireland, 'as handy as a small pot', and this is where it came from. A little three-legged one was awful handy for lifting

off and on compared to the big ones. The big ones could be very dangerous: they were so heavy that most women could not lift them off and on without the help of a man. If you weren't careful with the swing of the crane you could easily get a nasty burn. More dangerous than the swinging out of the crane was removing the pot from it once you'd got it out. Because the pots were nearly spherical, and they had just the three legs, they tumbled easily. Children were never allowed near the pots. In fact, the open fire was one of the hazards of young life. The old women were always terrified of accidents with the fire. If there was a granny in the house – and there usually was – she'd be sitting in the corner and saying to her daughter or daughter-in-law, 'Keep the child back from the fire, don't he fall in.' The granny's chair would be a sugan (seat made from straw rope). Some of these sugan chairs had armrests and if they had they were awful comfortable. Many an old lady ruled the household from such a throne. They saw everything, hence the saying: 'An eye in the corner is as good as ten around the house.'

The dresser was the most important item of furnishing. It had an open top part. In this open part was displayed all the best things possessed by the household. There were plates and dishes and maybe a china or Delft teapot. The open shelves had hooks from which hung cups and jugs. You could tell a lot about a family from the dresser. The 'good housekeeper' would have it shining; careless ones might have any old thing stuck up there. Behind the plates was a great place for hiding important bits of paper – letters from America, bills and receipts and maybe a special prayer to be said in times of illness, or a relic of some saint. A poem called 'The Old Woman of the Roads' by Padraic Colum (1888–1972) tells of a travelling woman who wishes she owned a house and dreams of having

A dresser filled with shining Delft,
Speckled and white and blue and brown.

The top of the dresser often held treasure, too – maybe a box camera or a tin box with medicine – Sloane's liniment, iodine and a bit of gauze and cream for burns.

Another important piece of furniture was the 'settle bed', a wooden bench seat closed in on three sides. The seat came off, revealing a box interior. You could sleep in it; it was awful snug, protected on all sides from draughts. Good houses had a pendulum clock – sometimes with chimes – and all houses had a picture of the Sacred Heart. In front of the picture a little paraffin lamp burned, the small flame from the wick shining through a red globe. Rosary beads hung close to the picture or from the shelf over the fireplace. At night the whole family went down on bended knee to say the rosary. If there were visitors they'd have to join in, too.

For children the rosary was very boring; the prayers had long words in them that they didn't understand and at the end there were all the 'trimmings', like the litany of the saints, prayers for good weather for the harvest or for rain to help the spuds, and prayers for departed relations. The young ones often got up to trickery during the rosary and if they got a fit of laughing it was awful hard to stop. Talk to anyone about saying the rosary and you will hear the same story: they were always bursting to laugh and terrified of their fathers if they did so. Many a father must have given up in anger and got up off his knees, asking God how he had ever raised such a 'pack of heathens' that couldn't even say their prayers without showing off their foolishness.

*

Pictures of the Sacred Heart and the Blessed Virgin were usually displayed in the kitchen. They could be repeated and added to in a bedroom as here in the home of Mrs. Buckley near Listowel in Co. Kerry.

Officially fires were for boiling pots and giving heat. They could turn into theatres of storytelling, too, with built in props of oil lamp, tongs, pots and pans. Even if there were a full house a latecomer could always pull up a chair and find a spot for himself.

The big table was wooden and scrubbed white and it was usually pushed in against a wall out of the way; when the men were called in from the field for the dinner it would be pulled out. All sat around it on stools. At dinner time the pot of potatoes would be tumbled straight out on to the table. They steamed mightily. As well as the 'spuds' there would be cabbage or turnips and maybe bacon. Red meat was very rare. A van did come around to farmhouses selling groceries: they took the eggs and butter and gave 'shop goods' in exchange. If you ordered it in advance they could bring red meat, but not many people could afford it.

When the table wasn't in use for dining it served many other purposes. The women kneaded the dough on it for making bread; they flattened out the material for dress making, and if there was a sewing machine it went on the kitchen table, too. In our house the big table was put to another, less obvious, use. On Saturday night my grandfather and uncles had their weekly shave for mass on Sunday morning. The kitchen table became their station of titivation. They filled enamel mugs with hot water and took the cut-throat razors out from the drawer of the dresser. Sharpening these instruments was an exercise in itself.

They had leather straps similar to those you sometimes still see in barber shops. These straps had a metal eye at one end and a handle at the other. The shaving men would hold the metal eye over a space between the boards that made up the surface of the table, then take the granny's scissors and stab it through the eye into the space so that the strap was held. Then, grasping the handle, they pulled the strap taut and sharpened the cut-throat by rubbing it up and down the smooth leather. They used a bristle shaving brush and soap to make a fine lather on the week's stubble and shaved it away, looking at themselves in a little mirror balanced against the mugs of steaming water. The whole process was a fine piece of performing art; the faces they made at themselves and the stroking of the razor on the strap constituted the best of mime.

All water had to be brought from the well. Sometimes the children or womenfolk drew the water in buckets, stooping against its weight across the fields. Sometimes it was brought in churns on the ass and cart but a lot depended on how accessible the well was. If it was near the *boreen* you could bring the water home on the ass and cart and that was awful handy; it saved a lot of work. If the well was in the middle of the field there was nothing for it but 'shank's mare': you had to draw it home on foot in buckets. Whichever way the water

Fishermen by the wall of the pier in Courtown Harbour, Co. Wexford.

Thatch was expensive to replace. If it weren't too bad it could be repaired and held down against the wind with heavy stones. This cottage was in Aran Island, Co. Galway.

came, what was to be used inside the house was kept in buckets which stood on low stools in the corner.

As well as the kitchen there might be a parlour. Not every house had one: in fact, a parlour was something of a distinction, a status symbol. People were only allowed into the parlour on rare occasions. Sometimes it even doubled as a bedroom for the granny.

Once a year the local priest said a mass in private houses around the parish. This was a big affair, known as 'the stations'. It took place in the parlour and if you didn't have a parlour you couldn't have the stations. The place had to be cleaned from top to bottom. It would have to be whitewashed and painted and the kitchen table had to be taken outside to the yard and scrubbed until it nearly wore away. The priest would use the table as an altar, and, even though it would be covered with many cloths, because of the importance attached to the sacrifice of the mass, the table had to be scrubbed as if someone was going to be operated on it. Aunts would come home from England to help with the stations; neighbours, too, came in and lent a hand. Bits and pieces of furniture and crockery would be borrowed all around.

While everyone scrubbed and polished and painted, all the time the question would be whispered around: 'I wonder who will eat with the priest?' This was the big prize. Only a few qualified and they had to be of some rank and station to be so rewarded. The size of the table in the parlour put a limit on numbers as well.

On the morning of the stations the place would be shining, spotless. All the neighbours would have gathered and the women would be inside the house preparing kettles and water and frying pans for the cooking of the breakfast. The men would be hanging around the yard in their good clothes, talking in small bunches with hushed voices.

They'd have caps on 'em and great clouds of smoke would rise up from the pipe smokers. Then the priest would arrive in a horse and trap, or, in later times, by car. He'd sweep out of whatever vehicle brought him and a silence would fall over the men. They'd doff their caps and 'his reverence' would wave a brief but expert blessing over them. They'd bless themselves and replace their caps while the priest dashed into the house, continuing the blessings as he went. He vested in the parlour. While he was doing that the women would be getting the men in from the yard, telling them to take off their caps again and get down on their knees and not be delaying the thing. The breakfast followed the mass.

The priest, and those deemed worthy to eat with him, had breakfast in the parlour; ordinary folk ate in the kitchen. There would be fried eggs, bacon, sausages and black and white pudding for the parlour people and boiled eggs for kitchen eaters. The men might get duck eggs, or, if not, they'd get two hen eggs. Everyone got jelly and custard afterwards. The jelly was always red. The conversation for weeks after would be about 'who ate with the priest'. Such a distinction did not weary with time; it could be as enduring as an academic qualification and probably more useful. It elevated one on the social ladder.

Outside the house in the farmyard there would be hens, ducks, geese, a pig or two poking around noisily with their snouts into everything, and maybe turkeys, though they were a delicate breed and required considerable care. They wandered a lot and there was always a danger from foxes. If the turkeys went missing an alarm would go up and any child around would be sent looking for the lost flock. Turkeys could travel some distance and might be found a field or two away. Geese were easier to rear. They were hardy and would eat almost anything, but I dreaded the geese; more correctly, I dreaded the gander. The female of the species seemed reasonably docile and didn't bother little boys too much, but the gander was a demon on webbed feet. He hated all children. An ornery creature, he probably hated all human beings, but he was cowardly so he specialised in terrorising the young of the species. I seem to have spent much of my youth trying to sneak past ganders unnoticed, every time with the same result. I'd creep up on the blind side of him, holding my breath.

Other than the demonic gander, garden fowl took kindly to children. The girl in the top picture has the guinea fowl practically eating out of her hands while the boy in the bottom one has a very special relationship with his rooster.

The hay was loaded onto a cart to be brought home. The 'gorsoon' in this picture is helping his father to tie the load down so it won't be blown away by the wind.

He'd pretend he hadn't noticed anything; he'd be there, head down sorting out edible stuff from the wet growth, looking all solicitous and cavalier sorting out tasty morsels for his harem. I'd be sure I'd got away. Then, in rejoicing, I'd get the tiniest bit careless, and breath.

That did it.

He'd abandon whatever he was up to, drop down the head, stretch out his neck, leave a hiss so low and long it sounded as if it came all the way from his tail and the chase would start. You'd think he'd not be capable of great speed. You'd think his webbed feet equipped him better for more aquatic pursuits than for sprinting but you'd be wrong. Ganders are white, yellow-billed lightening. There was no escaping him and that's the truth. My uncles, who were big and strong, could walk past him heads erect and he'd take not a pick of notice. A real coward. He had a mean eye, too, and it was red. I should know; many's the time I saw it up close.

The sow, too, could be dangerous. People were always saying the sow would eat a baby if she got half a chance. 'Don't she eat her own farrow?' they'd say. 'Of course, she'd eat a child if you weren't careful.' Although I was never afraid of the sow I always kept upwind of her because she could be awful smelly. She foraged around the yard, snouting into everything and making grunting noises ranging from disappointment to great satisfaction depending on what she had sorted out from the rubbish. It was true that she would eat her own farrow if she weren't watched. Many a night I remember my uncle staying up with a sow that was giving birth. He'd have to be there to take the bonhams away as soon as they were born in case she ate them. She could roll over on them, too, and crush or stifle them. In about 1950 farrowing pens were introduced to farms, into which they put the sow when she was having the young. It was a narrow wooden box just wide and long enough for her to stand up or lie down in. At the bottom there was a space about six inches off the ground through which the young bonhams could make their escape if the mother was inclined to do them harm. Even then someone had to stay with her until they were sure all the litter was safe. There could be anything up to thirteen in a litter. They used to pick the young ones according to strength and arrange them at the sow's teat. If you were going out to see the sow and her young someone would be sure to shout after you, 'put the strong bonham to the weak tit'.

Despite the sow's bad reputation I was attached to her. I liked pigs: there was something homely about them. I loved to feed the young ones. In the centre of the pig house there would be a round iron trough into which you tipped the bucket of feed. Before you got anywhere near it the pigs would be around you grunting loudly and nearly knocking you over. Then they fell almost into silence as they gobbled up the food; maybe the odd squeal as a weak one was forced out of his position. Then he'd jump up on the back of the bigger ones to get at the trough and there would be further commotion. When the pigs grew bigger they were too dangerous; you couldn't walk among them with the bucket of feed. You had to feed them over a wall. There was a section for the bigger pigs where the trough would be a long concrete one, part of the wall itself, and you dropped the feed into this trough, standing safely outside. When they heard the sound of the bucket coming they'd all rush to the trough. The place would be full of muck and manure and they'd be slipping around like skaters on ice. It was a real pleasure to watch pigs eating; they loved their

The man in the top picture is weaving in Co. Donegal while the bottom craftsman is covering hurling balls with a leather coat.

food. You couldn't afford to be too sentimental about the farmyard animals, though. In Ireland, as just about everywhere else, they all came to the same end. The little piglet weren't rescued from infanticide to live a long and full life, but just so they could provide bacon for the table at a later date.

The killing of the pig was no small affair. The unfortunate chosen one would be strung up in an outhouse and his throat cut. Some women, claiming unusual tenderness, used to make themselves scarce

When hay was cut it was left to 'bleach' in the sun before being gathered into cocks for convenience of collection and carrying home.

OPPOSITE:
(top) Other crops were bound in sheaves. Men with pikes pitched the sheaves to other men on top who arranged the load, to make it look tidy and secure.

(below) The threshing was the climax. Neighbours gathered from all around to help.

so they wouldn't hear the squealing. The others – braver – stood their ground in readiness for the work that followed. The pig was left hanging until every last drop of blood had drained out of him. Then he was cut into sections. The women rubbed rough salt into the pig pieces and steeped them in wooden barrels of water. The meat was left there for three weeks. The pig's intestines were removed and cleaned. Women prided themselves in this work; the hygiene of a household could be determined by how clean the guts were scraped before being stuffed with meal, blood and other ingredients needed to make puddings. These puddings were distributed to neighbours and relations; the children often took a piece of it to the teacher. Removed from the barrels, the salted meat was hung from the rafters in the kitchen and provided protein for the coming year. Visiting relations might be offered a slice of a hanging section by way of a parting gift.

A much bigger occasion than killing the pig was the threshing. First the crop had to be cut. This was done with a mowing machine. To give the mowing machine a place to start, men had to cut the first swathe around the headlands with scythes. The mowing machine did

the rest. Men followed behind the machine gathering the cut oats, barley or wheat into sheaves, then they tied each sheaf with a handful of what had been cut, first twisting it into a kind of rope. These sheaves were left standing in triangular stooks. When the stooks were taken home to the farmyard they had to be threshed to separate the grain from the straw.

In those days, threshing machines were a rarity and only a few big farmers had one, which they lent or rented out to others. Before tractors came in, the threshing machine was towed around by a steam engine with huge wheels, a funnel and a man on top shovelling in fuel. This man always had a black face. The steam engine was a sturdy machine. It resembled a prehistoric beast, a kind of dragon on wheels. It looked more threatening than the Wooden Horse of Troy. It belched out smoke and steam and made slow and ominous progress on those enormous wheels that dwarfed people. The threshing machine in tow was a spidery affair; it looked nervous in the wake of the beast that pulled it. It was made of wood and had many little bits and pieces; it shuddered along looking as if it was scared of falling apart from the insensitive dragging it was getting.

The threshing itself took a day or two, maybe three. Men came from all around. Neighbours sent a working man or a son to help. The thresher was placed near the stacks of sheaves that had been drawn in from the fields. The machine that towed it now stood beside it, giving it power via a rotating belt Men with pikes threw the sheaves to other men standing on top of the thresher who in turn fed the sheaves into an opening on the top. The machine did its shaking and shuddering and, lo and behold!, what went in as one piece came out in separate parts. The grain sped down chutes into waiting, hooked-on bags; the straw was juggled out through shuffling timber teeth.

Because this was hard work, a basin of porter was generally left at the doorstep of the house with a few mugs around it. The men drank from this to quench their thirst. 'Clear the throat from the old dust' they'd say before swallowing a mouthful, and then, ''tis thirsty work' they'd say, before taking a second. They laboured hard and joked loudly over the noise. There was an unspoken competition about who was strongest; everyone did his level best. The place was always full of rats:

The game of 'road bowling' called for as much knack as it did strength. A fellow who didn't look in peak condition could surprise you if he knew how to put spin on the iron ball.

OPPOSITE:
After every big event like threshing or 'the stations' there would be a dance in the house. Local musicans provided the music, everyone else danced and the thing could go on until morning.

The surface from which turf had been cut was called a bank. People were proud of their workmanship and a bank of turf should be smooth like the façade of a building. The men in the bottom picture are combining their efforts to make their rick of turf look good, too.

they would be inside in the sheaves, eating away for themselves. When the piking of the sheaves disturbed them they'd jump out. Sometimes the sheaf they jumped from would be mid-air and when they tried to get away they'd fly through the air before hitting the ground and scurrying off, running like crazy. A shout would go up and the men would try to kill them. The number of rats any one man killed was added to his tally of work and went towards his rating as a 'mighty man'. This was in no way official but everyone understood the competition. A few times I saw men throwing their pikes at rats in an effort to pin them to the ground, and a few times I saw them succeed.

In the middle of the day the threshers stopped to eat. They took off the caps before going into the house mumbling 'God bless all here' and sat on their stools around the kitchen table. The women emptied pots of spuds on to the middle of the table. Every man got a plate of bacon and cabbage and a mug of milk. There might be jelly afterwards. Red, as always.

When the threshing was finally done there would be a dance in the house. Some locals would play the violin or melodeon and maybe someone would play the spoons. They danced till morning. They did jigs and reels, 'The Siege of Ennis' and 'The Stack of Barley'. Everyone seemed to love dancing. When they started to swing to 'The Walls of Limerick' someone would give a screech and another would cry 'Around the house and mind the dresser' – there was always a danger of it coming tumbling down if someone broke loose in the spinning around. They might bump into the dresser and break the fine crockery.

No invitations were needed to these dances. It was understood that a threshing dance was for everyone to enjoy. There would be food and drink, the quantity depending on how good the harvest had been. One particular family (they had a name for wildness and extravagance) had a party that went on all night. The house was small and someone said they needed more room for the dancing, so they took the doors off their hinges and left the rooms into each other. They had two barrels of porter and no one went home until both of them were empty. The man who told this story ended with, 'Ah! Shure that family had no holt of the money.'

Turf was cut in summer time. The men used tools called 'slains' for the job. Each cut made a sod which was thrown to one side. The children footed – that is, arranged the sods in little pyramids to dry. At lunchtime the women brought cakes of bread and gallons of tea to the workers. There was no place like the bog for giving one an appetite and it was a great place to get a colour, too. You could get a tan from the bog that visitors to the Mediterranean would envy. When the turf was dry it was drawn home by horse, or ass, and cart. Then, it was

built into a rick in the yard. The neatness of the rick and the size of it said a lot about a family.

People living on off-shore islands had to use currachs to bring home the turf. It had to be well stacked, too, for the trip to prevent a capsize.

Cow's milk was sent to the creamery mostly but some was kept at home and skimmed. The cream was used for making butter; and the skimmed milk was fed to the pigs. The butter was made in a churn, which was like a wooden barrel with a lid. The lid had a hole in the middle and a 'dash' poked through the hole. The dash was a wooden handle that was pulled up and down for more than an hour until the butter appeared on top of the milk. The residue was called buttermilk and it was supposed to be good for any number of illnesses. There was a superstition about churning milk (making butter). If anyone called during the operation they had to take the dash and work it up and down for a while. If they didn't do that, the story went, there would be very bad luck and no butter would appear on the milk.

If country people washed the clothes by the river they had the bushes for hanging them out to dry. City dwellers, like here in Galway, if they hadn't a back yard had to make do with a bit of rope strung across the front of the house on the street.

There was no bad luck about washing clothes at the river. The women loved it. They didn't do it every week, only when they had a big wash with sheets and blankets a couple of times a year. The children loved it, too, and they were called in to help. They stamped barefoot on the sheets and blankets, for all the world like Frenchmen treading grapes. Afterwards the clean garments were left on bushes to dry. They were often left overnight; there was no fear of theft but the habit was not without danger. A cow could choke on a sock, or she could do something very nasty on clean sheets. The sheets and shirts themselves were often made from flour bags. In such a case, the miller's name would be washed away, leaving material that was the finest Irish linen.

*

Preparations for Christmas started in early December. The whitewash came out and everything got a daub – even the dog if he wasn't careful. The cleaning and preparations went on for two or three weeks and then it would be time for going to the market to sell and buy.

The turkeys were all fatted up, red in the head and in peak condition, little aware of the fate that lay in store. The creels were put on the cart and the horse was tackled. The birds' legs were tied together and they were loaded inside, eyes blinking in wonder and with a touch of apprehension. The men and women went together on this occasion. It was time to reap dividends and invest in new stock for the festive occasion. How much a pound the turkeys and geese might fetch was at the core of the debate among the women coming up to the season of goodwill. There would always be wild and extravagant rumours that they were going to be 'awful dear this Christmas', but that didn't usually materialize. Market forces prevailed long before

Well balanced donkeys taking home the turf.

As well as animal manure seaweed could be used to fertilise the land.

anyone had ever heard of Wall Street or the City; supply and demand fought it out until an equilibrium was reached at a price the selling women thought 'wasn't worth all the work and bother that went into minding them' and the buyer said was 'daylight robbery'.

Afterward the sellers went to the pub and part of the dividends were spent on bottles of stout and small ports. Most women didn't usually drink, but after selling the turkeys they might take a glass of port or two, and then the heads would be all red on them, like the turkeys they had sold. They'd be doing their best to appear steady and overserious as they coaxed the menfolk out of the place to do the rest of the Christmas shopping.

This, apart from the threshing, would be the biggest day of the year. The shop owner and the purchaser would be full of good cheer and merriment but they'd be studying form, too. They'd be weighing each other up and down more carefully than the assistant would be weighing out the goods on the scales. The owner would be estimating the value of the purchase and the customer would be wanting to make it look like he was in a buying frenzy. The reason was 'the Christmas present'. All customers got one. There was a ratio between what was bought and what present the shopkeeper gave.

Nearly everyone got a 'barm brack' (a light fruit cake). That was fairly standard. A Christmas pudding was rare, a tin of biscuits even more so. Packets of sultanas and raisins, on the other hand, were very common. They'd also give a bottle of port and a few bottles of Guinness, and nearly always tobacco for the men. But, on top of the present, no matter how mighty or humble the customer, would be a one-pound candle. It was always red and about eighteen inches long. It was the natural 'top piece' to the gift.

Irish folklore and culture thrived on the islands off Ireland, but life was tough and many of the islands were abandoned. The strong and healthy men in the top boat are evacuating Great Blasket Island in County Kerry. Those in the one below are fishing for shark off Achill. Achill and Aran remain populated and do a flourishing tourist trade. Irish is spoken on both islands; it is the lingua franca of Aran.

This final purchasing before the big day was itself called 'the Christmas'. So, after the selling of the turkeys and geese, the parents would arrive home with 'the Christmas'. Children were awful curious as to what was in the bags and boxes but they were kept from poking through them, the reason being 'Santa Claus' was in among the goodies. Just as the shopping was called after the feast, so what the merry man was going to bring down the chimney to good boys and girls was called after the man himself – 'the Santa Claus'.

Christmas Eve was a fast day, which meant no meat or poultry was allowed. Almost every one ate salted ling fish with white sauce on Christmas Eve. After that there would be either Christmas pudding or barm brack, depending on which the local shop had presented. Hard to believe perhaps, but there were no Christmas trees in Ireland until the 1970s or so: you could see them in Christmas cards sent from America and there were wreaths on the doors, but there was something suspect about them. They looked a bit pagan. Families tended to have holly – a piece with red berries over the Sacred Heart picture and the

Ordinary people had a goose for the Christmas dinner. The better off learned the American habit of dining on turkey on festive occasions. Buying one was women's business and they dressed appropriately for the important event.

calendar, a bit on the window sill, and maybe a couple of bits here and there on the dresser.

The most important item of Christmas decoration was that Christmas candle. A turnip or mangold would be cut in half and a hole made in it. The candle was then stuffed into the hole and firmed up with old paper. If there was crepe paper it was cut in strips, fringed and wrapped around the turnip. But the final touch was a bit of holly with red berries to be tied on the middle of the candle. When that was done all was ready for the lighting ceremony. This was a solemn, often emotional, occasion undertaken either by the oldest or youngest member of the family depending on the tradition of the place. I was the youngest in our family and for me it was the most important moment of the whole year. The adults often spoiled my big moment and, until much later, I never understood why. They often cried. Now, I know it was because they were thinking about lost relations, but I didn't understand that then. After I lit the candle we said some prayers, and, always, one of the adults would say, 'Go mbeirimid beo ar an am seo aris' ('May we be alive again at this time'). Then they did their crying.

On Christmas night the lighted candle was placed in the window so that if anyone was wandering the road without a place to stay for the night they would be guided by the candle. The idea came from Mary and Joseph looking for a place to stay on the first Christmas Night, but Santa used it, too, to find his way from house to house.

Christmas morning was always full of joy and laughter. Our stockings were filled with useful things. There was nearly always an orange down the toe which acted as ballast and bulk. There might not be a lot more, but the orange itself was a bright and beautiful thing and it lit up the eyes. Our Santa was very practical. He brought more clothes than toys. There were often shoes. I never did understand how he knew our sizes, but he did.

No doubt but that Santa was some powerful man.

Common goose buying was not quite as grandiose but it still called for costume – hats, furs and cravat. These Cork women wear them well and put on faces to go with them.

CHAPTER TWO

Wayside Wars and the Sally Rod

'We listened for birdsong, watched the rabbits run, gave chase but never caught them. But then, when we got within viewing distance of the schoolhouse, reality kicked in. Commerce came into play – a 'cut' of bread or a sup of milk could be exchanged for a page of sums. The expenditure was not only worth it; it was a necessity for healthy living. Our teacher did not understand the business that kept us from doing our homework.

   She occupied another world.'

Irish people used to be very sensitive to what was said about their country. They were a little unsure of themselves. They examined every utterance about their island to make sure there was no insult hidden in there. Criticism was not invited; nearly all comment was suspect. In this period of uncertainty I remember reading somewhere that Ireland was a small country of small houses with small windows and big families. I huffed for a little while, but then, seeing the truth in it, I laughed to myself and thought, they could have added 'small schools' as well.

In the towns and cities there were larger schools, but yesterday's Ireland was mostly rural. Towns were far apart and the majority of people lived in the country and acquired their education in the small schools.

Country schools were awful small and they were everywhere, on the side of every road. You could have schoolhouses just three or four miles apart. There were no school buses so everyone walked; that

Schools and the boys who went to them may have been small but the mugs they drank out of were big. They were sometimes called 'ponnies'. The same 'ponnies' went to the bog when the men were cutting turf.

must be the reason why there were so many schools. And, like they said about the houses and windows, the schools were very small, too. Some were of just one room but mostly they were of two: one for young children from the ages of four to about six or seven, and the other for 'the big boys and girls'. These rooms were separated by a partition. It might be raised off the ground a bit or it could be one of those concertinaed ones that folded back to make the whole lot into one big room for special occasions, as, for example, when the priest was coming.

If there were two rooms there had to be two teachers. There would be a headmaster or headmistress and his or her assistant. School teaching was one of the few areas where there was something close to gender equity: the top position could be held by a man or a woman. There was often an awful divide between the two teachers. Heads

"And still they gazed, and still their wonder grew, That one small head could carry all he knew." This is how Oliver Goldsmith describes the Village Schoolmaster in his epic poem, 'The Deserted Village'. These boys like anxious vessels are ready to receive part of the great knowledge.

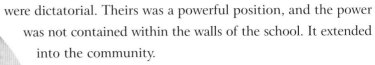

Sitting in a row on the wall. The good wellingtons and the caps suggest this was a posed picture. Maybe taken to send to the Yanks to inspire them to send more clothes.

were dictatorial. Theirs was a powerful position, and the power was not contained within the walls of the school. It extended into the community.

What I heard from my parents about their school days differed little from what I experienced myself. Yet I am sure my experiences of school have no similarity at all to what goes on inside the fine educational edifices of today. Things did not change much between 1900 and 1960. After that, however, there was a complete overhaul; today's children would find it hard to believe what it was like.

What went on inside all small schools was probably similar, I believe. The one I went to was a one-teacher establishment on the side of a quiet country road. It was in a district called Camphire, five miles from the nearest town, Cappoquin, in County Waterford.

A lady reigned over that school.

The focal point of the school was the open fire. The teacher sat in its vicinity and children were summoned to it, for instruction and examination. Our mistress had an arc drawn in chalk on the wooden floor around the fire. When we were called up for our lessons we had to toe this line. The idea was to keep us back a bit from the flame – not so much from its danger as from its comfort – and not to block the heat too much from the rest of the room; or from her.

The trip to school was an excursion itself. We walked through the fields from the house and met up with other school-bound children at the crossroads. I always thought the ones who lived on the road, and hadn't to cross the fields first to get there, were a bit superior to us. I thought they were smarter because they saw more things and people moving about. They seemed less afraid than those of us who lived up lanes and across the fields. They were what we would nowadays call streetwise.

After meeting we walked together the couple of miles to school. Once you got out on the road it was a fairly straight way, but we made it long for ourselves by running back and forth. We travelled in small groups separated by twenty or thirty yards. There was nearly always some minor war afoot, someone not talking to someone else. Who you walked with depended on the alliance you were in. It was a matter that called for much diplomacy. Sometimes allegiances could change a few times on one trip. An ally of the first half-mile could turn into a bitter enemy by the second, so there was much toing and froing to stay in the appropriate camp.

These conflicts often brought on other crises.

I had very strong older sisters who had little respect for the right of independent thought. They thought I should follow their lead. My innate sense of justice was often subordinated to their power of visual persuasion. A look from them might not exactly kill but it did rather direct one. On the frequent occasions they split, and occupied opposing groups, I suffered huge internal conflicts. My discretion, valour and righteousness fought it out inside, while my outward senses had to steer a course fraught with danger. They were big strong girls.

In times of peace the trip was pure adventure. In summer we were barefoot. We picked berries and kicked at tall grass to get the insects into flight, or rout. We watched animals. We jumped ditches to check things were the same on other side. We searched out birds' nests and looked for fish in streams. An eel lived under a

Something says these children came from a different class; even the dog looks more for petting than working around a farm.

stone: the older ones said he could take your toe off with one bite. He looked evil enough. He had a mean eye and wriggled like a serpent – could be related to the one which made Adam and Eve eat the apple.

We listened for birdsong, watched the rabbits run, gave chase but never caught them. But then, when we got within viewing distance of the schoolhouse, reality kicked in. All outward evidence – berry stains around the mouth, a bloodied knee or torn trousers – had to be camouflaged, and, most important of all, exercise had to be copied. Commerce came into play – a 'cut' of bread or a sup of milk could be

exchanged for a page of sums. The expenditure was not only worth it; it was a necessity for healthy living. Our teacher did not understand the business that kept us from doing our homework.

She occupied another world. She'd not understand the things we thought important. Hers was a world of books with dog ears, of covered copybooks with neat writing and of questions promptly 'and correctly!' answered. What she and we thought important were miles apart.

Once I tried to bridge that gap.

I had reached the age of eight. The sisters had moved on and I had arrived at some sort of self-determination. I sometimes went alone to school. One morning in May I heard the cuckoo. I must have just arrived at a new level of aural perception because it excited me like nothing I had heard before. I dropped the satchel and went in pursuit of that haunting sound. Failing to find it, I picked up my satchel and hurried off to school. Though I ran all the way, I couldn't make up lost time.

I was late.

I told the teacher what had happened, that I had heard the cuckoo and tried to see it. To me it was so momentous I thought that even she would have to understand.

No.

She wasn't impressed. She looked at me over her wire-rimmed spectacles Her untidy bun trembling with age and indignity she trebled, 'and I suppose you know that that bird builds no nest?' I didn't but it did not reduce him in my estimation. If I could make a sound like that I wouldn't be wasting my time building nests either.

'And do you know why that bird builds no nest?'

'No, ma'am.'

My heart sank as she went on to explain how the cuckoo was late for the Lord's lesson in nest building. She stole all the joy from what I had heard. She told me I was like the cuckoo. She said the reason he could not build a nest was because he was late for the Lord's instruction on how to do it. He was late, she said, because he was

When push comes to shove the donkey will always have his way. When an ass decides which way he is going to go you might as well give up trying to change his mind.

Black and white and boss all over. Nuns carried even more authority than ordinary teachers. These were times when 'disruptive pupils' weren't yet invented.

proud of his own voice and wasted his time 'showing off' on his way to the nest-building lesson. He stopped at every flower on the way to awaken it with his cuckoo call. I thought this was wonderful but our teacher said he shouldn't be doing it. She said he was 'tardy'.

'Just like you,' she said. 'Stopping on his way to instruction, and forgetting to see to the important things in life.'

Maybe I was 'tardy' but I learned an important lesson that day: you can't put a young head on old shoulders.

School was a busy place. Catechism was the most important subject. It had to be learned by heart and it was not to be understood. Some of the words were not to be known, they were just to be said. For example: 'Sixth, thou shalt not commit "adultery".' That word 'adultery' was not to be used other than in reciting the commandments. It was an 'adult' word; it only concerned big people. We had to know the commandments and be able to say them, but it was not necessary to understand what we were saying. The teacher would tell us what we should and shouldn't do.

We were to have no impure thoughts.

'What is impure thoughts, ma'am?'

'Never mind the impertinent questions, do what you are told; no impure thoughts words, deeds or actions, and say your prayers.'

But the prayers, as we shall see in a subsequent chapter, posed their own problems. Particularly the 'Hail Mary' and its apparent reference to 'a monk swimmin''. Such an interpretation seemed perfectly reasonable because monks fell within the context of holy things like prayer, and the 'swimmin'' could be something to do with Jesus and baptizing John in the river. But after the 'impure thoughts' fracas we dared not ask for further guidance.

The tables, too, were problematic. No great difficulty with words here, straightforward and scientific; the problem was breaking them down to single lines. They were easy when you took a run at them:

Six ones are six.
Six twos are twelve.
Six threes are eighteen.
Six fours …

Making a great effort at writing Irish under the stern gaze of the master, of course.

All very well until she pounced: 'Six sevens? Quickly!' Where were you then and you only knowing them like a poem? She expected you to be able to break into the middle as if every line were detached from the one before it. The good lady who taught us knew nothing about the rhythm of tables. She believed in making things difficult.

With the founding of the Irish Free State the Irish language became a compulsory subject. From 1922 on, by law one-third of all school time had to be spent on Irish. Teachers had to be fluent in the native language. Most of them were zealous about the native tongue. Apart from the time spent at Irish as a subject, much of whatever else went on in class was conducted in Irish, too.

Independent thought was not encouraged, so all read from the same hymn sheet.

OPPOSITE:
Children were taught at school that the grace they received from the sacraments was the most important thing about the First Holy Communion and the Confirmation. They believed it. But secretly among themselves they also thought the taking of the photos after was of great moment, too.

At my school our lady took advantage of this; she loved to confuse us bilingually. We studied Irish and English and she switched tongues with ease – and malice. Just when you thought you had the hang of what she was driving at in English she'd switch to *'an teanga dhuchais'* (native tongue). We read and wrote in Irish and in English. There was a storybook for each; the Irish one was the more colourful but the characters were unlikely. Names like 'Art' and 'Una', names we never met in real life back then. They weren't real, and the teacher in the Irish book was smiling and benign – definitely fiction.

We wrote in two languages as well and that involved pen and ink. The ink had to be made. This was quite an operation; it was undertaken about once a fortnight. The 'good boys and girls' would be picked for going across the fields, to the stream, for the water. They brought it back in earthenware jars. The teacher took out the tin of ink powder and measured an amount carefully into a jar. Then the strong boys were given the job of shaking the potion until it became ink. The girls, in the meantime, would have taken the inkwells out of the desks and emptied the congealed contents into the bushes at the end of the playground. They washed the little white glass containers and replenished them with the new brew.

That teacher seemed infallible but sometimes she erred. Once she picked a boy to go for the water who couldn't do any job without getting up to some mischief. He had done something good and she thought he had turned over a new leaf. Age does not understand how set young boys can be in their wicked ways.

He brought back more than water.

She went through the process of adding the powder and getting it shaken and having it distributed into the clean inkwells. It didn't flow smoothly. There were lumps in it. On close examination some of the lumps were found to have life – they wriggled. The boy had brought back the water all right but he had also caught plenty of minnows and put them in the jar as well.

Now and then the priest came around to examine the catechism. He was nicer than the teacher and understood mistakes. He'd help you out with the answer. Sometimes you'd know it anyway, but the teacher would be standing there behind him with that awful hard face – she'd be staring iron rods at you and you couldn't think of a thing. I think the priest would know because if you watched his mouth he'd be moving it in the shape of the words. He was a bit afraid of her, too. I think even the bishop had heard about her.

Confirmation was a most important sacrament. She told us it would 'finish us off' as Christians. She said the Holy Communion was really only a preparation for becoming a full Christian – that happened with the Confirmation. It took the whole year to prepare. As well as the Ten Commandments you had to learn the Six Precepts of the Church, and what was forbidden, and what was commanded, by each one. There were other bits and pieces, too, which I have now forgotten, but it took an awful lot of effort. As the big day approached the parents were worried about the clothes that had to be bought; and the children worried about what they might be made to wear.

'I want shoes.'

Coming home from the Confirmation in Carraroe Co. Galway. The shawls might get another outing next Sunday for the mass but the white dress and veil was destined for mothballs until the next girl in the family was big enough to be confirmed.

'You'll wear strong boots that will last you the winter.'

All the teacher had to think about was the catechism and the bishop. 'If you let me down in front of the bishop ...' She didn't have to finish it; we knew what was in store. Trying times. But when it came it was much easier than she had said. She told us he would be asking the hardest questions, the ones with all the words that we didn't understand. But he didn't. He asked the easiest ones of all, the ones everyone knew.

'Who made the world?'

Simple stuff. So easy most of us were afraid there was a catch. But even at that didn't Peter Ahern (the fellow who put the minnows in the ink) make a mistake?

'Who is God?' the bishop asked.

Nothing.

'God is our F-a-t-h ...,' the bishop prompted.

Nothing.

'God is our Father in Heaven, isn't that right?'

'No, sir, my father is down the back of the chapel.'

But the bishop let him off; he pretended he hadn't heard. He gave us all a tap on the cheek, let us kiss his ring, and told us we were now 'strong and perfect Christians and soldiers of Jesus Christ'.

National School teachers (as teachers at these primary level schools were called) were very important people in the community. They rated with the priests. They were considered to be both intelligent and knowledgeable. They wrote letters for people and gave advice about all sorts of matters. Until the thirties they were not interfered with. They ran their schools as they liked. Some of these National Schools had a wide range of subjects as a result. If a National teacher had a particular interest he or she could indulge it in his own little kingdom of the National School. They might be teaching geography of far off places, maybe Africa if they had a son on the missions there, or a bit of botany or nature study if there was something they fancied themselves. Lady teachers often taught laundry, sewing, cooking, knitting and lace making. Some teachers used the students to cut their own turf or help with other chores, such as looking after their donkeys or ponies. But as the Irish Free State matured the Department of Education started to take greater control of what was happening within the schools. With the

advent of compulsory Irish, and the amount of time that had to be devoted to the language, teachers' autonomy diminished. The Department of Education wanted to keep a track of what exactly was going on in the classrooms. For this purposes, *cigires* were invented. That is the Irish word for inspectors.

Teachers feared *cigires* as much, or more, than pupils feared the bishop and his catechism questions.

They had cars – that's how important they were. They roamed the countryside, sneaking up on schools trying to find teachers doing something they shouldn't be doing. Teachers had a network going.

The catechism thought that Confirmation made children strong and perfect Christians and soldiers of Jesus Christ. This new army of Connemara Christians looks like it is lined out for inspection.

They sent messages to each other – 'he was here yesterday, he might be coming your way'. Our lady was so bad I think she didn't trust the network; she thought the others might be glad to catch her out, and maybe she was right. When she thought the inspector was in the district she had one boy sitting up on the windowsill keeping an eye on the road. 'If you see a car coming round that corner, hop down straight away and tell me, *tuigeann tu?*' ('you understand?').

We understood all right. The window was a great station. It faced into the sun and it was awful cosy and comfortable and you saw all that was going on in the road. The neighbours knew the trick she was up to. They'd see us sitting up on the window and they'd try to make us laugh. They'd pull faces and move their bodies to imitate cows scratching against something. Then they'd shake with the laughing in the safety of the outside world. They knew that we inside couldn't react. She'd kill us.

Fortunately it didn't happen on my watch. It was John-Joe McGrath's. He was a good and conscientious boy who usually made no mistakes and took no risks, not a bit like Peter Ahern. But, like any little boy, he got tired every now and then. On the day it happened 'twas a lovely day. The sun was high in the sky. It poured through the window and beamed down on John-Joe. He was fat and vulnerable to its comfort.

He nodded off.

The *cigire* came round the corner and no one knew. He didn't even knock on the door; he came straight in. The place was upside down. It never was as bad before. One class was on its way back to the desk and another making its way up to her when in he came.

'*Cad ta ar suil anseo?*' ('What is going on here?') he asked.

Well, you'd want to see her. Pale

Donkey and friend bring home the turf.

she went. The stray hairs stood up, the glasses nearly cracked with the frightened eyes glaring through them, like hot pokers. She was so confused she didn't know what to say. She was trying to smile and talk in Irish to make him happy (*cigires* loved Irish) but it came out all blubbering. Then he saw John-Joe in the window and he said in Irish:

'What is that child doing sitting there on the window?'

'Oh-h-h!' she stuttered 'that, *cigire*, is a delicate child; he needs the sun, his mother said he was to sit in the sun.'

Well, I nearly laughed; what anyone's mother said had no effect on this woman, but she pretended that John-Joe was sitting there because his mother said so.

I don't think he believed her. He shot questions all around the place and we made an awful show of answering. He was very red and he went up close to her and said more stuff in Irish. She got red, too; she was smiling away but you could see through it a mile off – she was in a panic. I think they could lose their fine jobs if the *cigire* said so.

Well, after that John-Joe was a delicate boy all right. She hauled

Before Riverdance children learned how to do jigs, reels and hornpipes in Driminagh National School 1951. Backs were straight, hands down by the sides and the teacher counted out the steps: 1 – 2– 3 – 4 –5 – 6 – 7 and a 1–2–3 and a 1– 2–3…

him down from the window and started lashing out at him with her bony hands. Then, in case she'd hurt herself, she sent him out for a 'sally rod'. She gave him a knife she kept in her desk and she said, 'Go out there and cut me a nice sally rod. I'll show you manners. You won't fall asleep in the sun when I'm finished with you.'

In the days when this lady became a teacher the way they did it was this. The most able student, or maybe two, was picked out in sixth or seventh class. Sixth or seventh depended on the school, some schools had six classes, others seven. The selected ones became monitors. They became apprentices to the teacher; they assisted with ruling copybooks, marking exercises and teaching the younger ones. After this they went on to some college where they took a formal qualification. I don't know if it was in the college or from the teachers they were apprenticed to that they learned how to slap; all I know is that they learned it well. Every teacher I knew and every one I heard about from friends was great at the slapping. You wouldn't think our lady would be any good at a thing like that but you'd be wrong. You should have seen her in action. To give her her due she didn't do much of it – not nearly as much as others I heard of – but when she did she could fairly wield that sally rod. A sally is a tree, and it sprouts twigs that are straight, vicious and swishy. When she was laying into John-Joe for falling asleep on the window you'd hear that swish no matter how you tried to cover up your ears. She gave him six strokes, three on each hand. This was a moderate amount – many teachers gave six on each hand but our lady never exceeded a total of six.

That was enough. Poor John-Joe was destroyed after it. In the playground we talked about it and there was something close to a protest. We thought it was very unjust and considered reporting the matter to our parents. However, when the heat went out of us, we decided it might not be the wisest course of action to take: it was likely they would take her side, for they always did. We concluded the chances were that John-Joe's parents would give him another few belts if they found out he had done something wrong. Parents had great faith in the teachers.

We discussed other ways of defeating her. We had all heard

Released from class to play the children invented games. Whatever they were at the laugh was always loud.

that if you put a horsehair across your palm the sally rod would snap in half. It wasn't an immediate remedy for poor John-Joe but it did help him recover. His father had a horse and he said he would collect all the hairs he could. We gloated in what would happen the next time she tried to do the slapping.

I must say the lady could teach. Her methods were not of today; they weren't very 'student centred'. Today everyone says education has to be student centred. Our teacher's method worked. I can still recite every line of poetry we learned. I nearly remember all the catechism, too, and even though I don't follow it to the letter I sometimes find it a useful reference point. And I know that a horsehair across your palm makes no impact on a sally rod.

No place better than up a tree to get a birds eye view of things. Here they are watching horses at the point-to-point races in Kanturk, Co. Cork.

OPPOSITE:
Hurling is a game of great skill. They say that more than in any other sport it is important to keep your eye on the ball and be ready to give it a flick with the hurling stick when it drops down to you.

The lady liked me, and, despite all, I must say the affection was somewhat reciprocated. The old monitor system had gone but she didn't let it die in her school. She had many monitors. The best one from sixth class instructed the fifth, while the best from that class taught what he had previously learned to the ones below him. When I came to sixth she chose me as her chief assistant; of course, she never gave me the title or any recognition but it was understood. To teach something you had to know it very well; having to tell it to someone else was a great incentive to greater understanding. I myself went on to be a teacher and I think my calling to that career was in no small way inspired by the lady I feared so much.

*

A disproportionate part of my youth was summer and sunshine. Like all people, I remember more sunny days, and summer seasons than frost and winter. Whatever internal mechanism controls our memory gives preference to the happy times, and a good thing that is, too. But there were winters. They were cold. We didn't go barefoot then, no indeed; on with the boots with the rows of studs on the soles to protect the leather. There was frost on the ditches and on the grass and ice on the puddles and the ponds. It all had to be tested for strength. If it were thin enough we broke it up with pebbles and it was strong enough to resist our efforts we tried it further. We walked on it. If it didn't crack and grumble then we took to skating. The studs on the boots were great for that. You'd leave marks on the ice, and pride yourself in the art created – swirls and scrapes. Jack Frost himself would have painted the windowpanes of the school with a filigree of fine ice when we got to it.

Every school had an open fire, the only heating there was for the entire school. Different schools had different systems for providing the firing. Our lady instructed us to pick *cipins* (little sticks) on the way to school. This we did (she was not to be disobeyed). It was a bad job on a cold morning, 'twould freeze the fingers off of you. And when you had a gwal (bundle) in your arms 'twas hard to blow on the fingers to make 'em warm.

Picking *cipins* was no amateur's job. You could not do it without

PAGES 68–9:
The journey home from school was leisurely. This is in Dooagh, Achill, Co. Mayo.

some science. You got to know the ones that lit well. You got to appreciate them like any other work of art. You developed a kind of discrimination in the world of little sticks: green, straight ones with shiny bark were no good; they had to be knurled and brittle before they'd pass our test. And of course everyone knew 'sally' would never burn, and it could be put to other uses, too. We'd never pick up a 'sally'. Bad enough when you had to cut one from the tree at her request.

When we got to the school without bundles (in winter time she arrived the same time as us) we tore up old copybooks, kept over the years, and put them under the grate. Sometimes you'd come across one belonging to someone you knew – a grown-up who'd been to the place years earlier – and you'd finger through it to see how good or bad he was. The sticks were put on top of the torn copybooks and the lady herself performed the lighting ceremony; she struck the match.

The heat was officially switched on!

The journey home from school was more leisurely than the one going, especially in summer when the days were long and sunny. We talked about the day and how it had gone. We checked out the birds nest, first for eggs and then for young. We watched them grow from little more than open mouths to shaky, half-feathered bits of wobbly flight. Each nest had an owner – the one who saw it first. Others were allowed to look inside only at the owner's say-so. If someone took the chance of looking without asking, another feud could erupt. I think bird's nests were the biggest cause of strife. Other bits of nature were taken into private ownership, too. 'That's my hawthorn! Who gave you the right to eat the berries from my bush.'

'What makes it your bush?'

'I saw it first.'

'No you didn't.'

'Yes I did.'

'Didn't.'

'Did.'

So the beginnings of another skirmish and dividing into ranks.

Sometimes there could be a major event like a stray bull. They were

Travelling people always had a big animal following: horses, ponies, jennets, mules, donkeys, goats and dogs. The rabbit suspended here, seemingly, did not follow of his own accord; he needed a little persuasion to come along.

awful dangerous but there was nothing better than a stray bull to mend the broken friendships. We had to unite against a common enemy. Farmers, too, could be a reason to close rank. We crossed their fields in search of things like mushrooms. If they gave chase past enmities were put away. There was nothing like a common cause to unite us boys and girls. We had to protect our own kind against the bullying world of stray bulls and 'big people' who understood very little.

Every road to school had an 'odd lady'. Ours we called 'the witch': she was little more than a bundle of rags tied in the middle, with a black hat on her head winter and summer. She kept goats which she grazed on the side of the road. We'd cross the ditch to avoid her. They said she had the evil eye and, if she looked at you, you could turn into a witch yourself. Who'd want that? The goats were strange looking creatures, too, and they had beards. No doubt some distant relation of the devil. And they had an eye that'd pierce you with its glassiness – evil, too.

The time came and we had to move on. Some completed their education at National School. You had to attend until you were fourteen. That is why some schools had a seventh class. It was a kind of 'finishing school' for those who were going no further. If they were intelligent the seventh class was used to good purpose, but if not, if

The lady may be bent by time but it hasn't impacted her belongingness to the place. She looks as much part of Connemara as do the cottage and the hill.

they had no interest and were just marking time to satisfy the requirement of the law, then these big ones were used for cleaning the grounds or seeing to the needs of the teacher's pony during the day.

Secondary schools were a lot more rare and you'd only find them in big towns. That meant you had to have a bicycle to get to them but such machines were rare. Many an intelligent person's education came to a premature ending for lack of a bicycle. People walked up to six or seven miles to get to a secondary school. If it was further away you had to have a bike.

Aunts or uncles who lived in the city or in a big town might take a niece or nephew in to allow them to go to school there. My own mother got her education in this way. She had an uncle in Cork with a good job in the civil service. His wife was a city woman and did not understand country ways. She had no children herself and kept a very 'proper' house. My mother used to tell about her first meal in this house. The aunt poured the tea. When my mother thought she had enough she said: 'Wheeeee …' The aunt was shocked; she said, 'Isn't that what you say to a donkey, Nora!' It was, of course, but, truth is, country people communicated with their animals as effectively as they did with their family.

The secondary schools could be tough. I was lucky. I went to a school run by Cistercian monks on the side of a hill in County Waterford. These men lived an austere life. They rose at 2 a.m., sang psalms, lauds, matins and vespers, worked in the fields and went to bed again at seven. But they didn't impose the rigours of their chosen life on us. They were liberal beyond their times; they were happy in themselves and made life happy for us, too.

But there were others whose cruelty knew no bounds. Christian brothers and nuns whose aspirations to Christianity were not echoed in the way they treated students.

Oliver Goldsmith (1728–74) was born in Pallas, County Longford, the son of a Protestant vicar of that village. He revisited his birthplace in 1770, four years before his death, and wrote his famous poem 'The Deserted Village'. Although it was written nearly two hundred years before the period under discussion, his description of the schoolmaster could easily fit that of a National teacher in Ireland in the forties.

He talks about the arguments between the vicar and the schoolmaster: 'Words of learned length and thundering sound, amazed the gazing rustics ranged around.'

We learn from his beautiful poem that in Goldsmith's time the teacher did not spare the rod either. In the twilight of his life, Goldsmith forgave the teacher for his harshness. He said: '... or if severe in aught the love he bore for learning was at fault'. Many pupils of my father's and my own generation would not agree.

It doesn't do to dwell on such unpleasantness. What most people remember is the wondrous trip to school and the journey home. It was a nature trail we undertook each morning with satchelful of books and bread. On the final lap home through the field we'd stop by the stream to soak our tired feet. Then, nearing the house, we'd see the old sheep dog running to welcome us home. I am sure that dog could read the time.

Technical Schools taught trades as well as academic subjects. They were staffed by lay people and they were sometimes mixed. Priests called to see things religious weren't neglected.

CHAPTER THREE

Buddhist Donkeys, Club Orange and the Rose of Tralee

'Donkeys have no illusions about themselves; they know exactly who and what they are and they have no hang-ups about it. Human beings (those who don't know donkeys personally) assign them to a lowly rank, but that doesn't bother donkeys. They know what they know and they make no effort to convert people to more correct thinking. They let people struggle on under the illusion they are superior. Donkeys probably think people are asses.'

Throughout Ireland horses were very precious and they were used with love and respect. They were the ones that did the work, ploughing, harrowing, mowing, bringing home the hay, and they were the only means of transport to go for the help of a doctor or priest in times of emergency. In those old days people knew all the horses around the place; they'd know even at a distance which horse was galloping the road. Each horse had a slightly different sound to his gallop.

I heard that there was always great speculation if a horse was heard passing at an unusual time. First people would cock their ear to figure out whose horse it was, and when they had that established they busied themselves wondering where it was going. If it were galloping at great speed an emergency was assumed. If it was the doctor's horse they knew someone was sick and if it were the priest's horse they suspected someone was very sick indeed, because they wouldn't be bothering the priest unless the person needed anointing. And the sick were only anointed if there was no hope for them.

The other person who had a horse was the solicitor and if he was heard going down the road it aroused acute interest, especially if the doctor had already gone by. It was assumed the sick person had made no will and those who stood to benefit were trying to get 'the place signed over' before the dying. Solicitors were always associated with 'signing over'.

Apart from horses, all animals were important to people living in the country. There were cows, bulls and bullocks, rams, ewes and their lambs, boars, sows and bonhams. And there was the donkey.

The donkey was an important beast, one not to be underestimated. Donkeys have no illusions about themselves; they know exactly who and what they are and they have no hang-ups about it. Human beings (those who don't know donkeys personally) assign them to a lowly rank, but that doesn't bother donkeys. They know what they know and they make no effort to convert people to more correct thinking. They let people struggle on under the illusion they are superior. Donkeys probably think people are asses.

Donkeys always live near the house and farmyard. They're usually there in the field beside the house. Most of the time they are just

Small donkey takes big man where he (small donkey) wants to go.

chewing away but every now and then you will see them raise their head and have a look around. You wouldn't put an awful lot of pass on this look if you didn't have 'donkey sense', but if you did you'd know a donkey can take in as much in half a minute with his head and ears up as you or I would do in a week in school. They are reading everything. Another thing is that they are unprejudiced about information. They don't make judgements; they just accept things as they are and store them away as information that will influence their future living. If animals had religion, donkeys would be Buddhists.

Horses knew when hoofs were in good hands. Good blacksmiths said quiet things to the animals that soothed them while they were putting new shoes on them.

People paid little attention to donkey's sensitivities, they talked over their heads.

PAGES 78-9:
Horse drawn carts to the left, motorised vehicles to the right. That seems to be the parking regulations for this fair at Midleton in Co. Cork.

They accept; they don't analyse and they don't bother themselves trying to change things. What is is, as far as the donkey is concerned. They don't let reality impinge on their own *modus operandi* – the donkey will do what the donkey wants to do, irrespective of the vagaries of a fickle human world. The donkey acts with conviction.

From the field beside the house they don't look as if they are taking any notice of anything. They don't look over that gate too much. They don't have to. The donkey is hearing everything. Those noble ears on top of his head are not just to make him look beautiful – they are veritable antennae. They were receiving signals long before Marconi ever thought of the wireless. The donkey hears you getting up in the morning (or, rather, heard; unfortunately, most of what I write about him should be in the past tense but I cannot deal with the sad reality that he is practically no more). He knows when you have milked the cow and he knows when his time has come to take the milk to the creamery. When you are ready the donkey will be

ready. Standing there at the gate waiting for you to open it and take him in to tackle him for the trip.

The donkey had only hoofs but he gave you the feeling that the front two were actually hands. You got the impression that, if he wanted to, he could put on his own harness. He acted like he let you do it because it was 'human work'. He did give assistance. He'd shake his mane and tail to tell you when things were right and comfortable and if you did it wrong, or made something uncomfortably tight, he'd paw the ground with a hoof. That was the first time you made a mistake; if you did it twice he'd lash out with his tail, and you wouldn't want to get a swipe of that. For all his small stature the donkey's tail packed a punch. And when he was ready he took you to the creamery.

He made all the decisions. He decided the pace, the route and the homeward journey. Sometimes people used to linger at the creamery, talking. The donkey wouldn't wait. When he had the business of delivering the milk done, he started the journey home. You could

Donkeys carried loads for people if they knew the people couldn't do it for themselves.

Milk was delivered in churns to the creamery. Horses and donkeys knew the procedure so well they could be left to themselves in the queue. The people supposed to be in charge of them were away talking.

follow when you liked, but your wishes made no impact on him. If donkeys could open gates I think they would have run farms on their own. Maybe they could open gates; they just didn't want people to know – too much would be expected of them.

There were other animals: cows to give calves and milk, bulls to father the calves, bulls which were made bullocks to cut down on their libido and give meat instead of making love, and there were ewes, rams, boars, sows and bonhams. There was much work and satisfaction surrounding animal life. A cow stuck in the bog would bring neighbours from miles to give help getting her out. Not everyone had a bull so bringing the cow to the bull could turn into quite a social outing. Sows visiting boars could also be an excuse for a gathering and the dipping of the sheep had a great festive air to it, too. The sheep themselves played a dramatic role in the dipping; you'd think they knew they had an audience. They performed. They skated around the wet and messy area where the dip was, they struggled

When they were being dipped a sheep's eye could give off as much emotion as a diva in the throes of anguish.

against being cornered and caught and, when they were finally dipped in the liquid, their eyes gave off as much emotion as a diva in the throes of anguish.

*

Fair days were invented for animals. Every decent sized town had a fair day each month. Animals were brought to fair to be sold. When we were children going to school in Tallow, County Waterford, in 1950, we'd know it was fair day because the road would be covered in dung. The farmers, jobbers, drovers and dealers would all have gone long before us – they went off at five or six in the morning – but the dung the animals dropped on the way would still be there when we went to school.

Some of our fathers and uncles would have gone off early and we'd be telling each other what we were selling or buying. I was always a bit afraid on fair days, for a number of reasons. Sometimes on the way home there would be fellows riding horses and they could be wild with

As well as singing, dancing and drinking they also sold horses at Puck Fair in Killorglin, Co. Kerry.

drink. You'd never know what way a drunk man on a horse might go. They might be going awful fast and the horse always knew when the rider was drunk. They'd be foaming at the mouth with the stress of it. And a foaming horse was a dangerous thing. Horses' eyes are usually wells of contentment but if they are being ridden by drunken men the eyes take on a wild appearance and show the whites. Horses could rear up, too, and if they did you never knew where they might bring their hooves down.

Drovers were usually quiet men, a breed apart. Their job was to drive the stock, usually cattle, to the home of the buyer. They never seemed to like the company of other men; they were almost always alone, just themselves and the animals they were driving. They were thinking men, maybe even dreamers. Padraic Colum wrote a poem about them called 'The Drover'. From it we get a glimpse of what the drover might have had on his mind as he travelled the roads of Ireland:

Then the wet, winding roads,
Brown bogs with black water,
But my thoughts on white ships
And the King of Spain's daughter.

Farmers all knew their own beasts; some men were better than others at this, but I heard that a good drover would get to know each animal in no time. I also heard that even if he picked up forty animals he had to drive from one place

At Cahermee Fair 1950 all the horses have shiny coats. Moneyed men wore suits and hats. Some wore waistcoats to hang their thumbs in. Other men wore caps, looked on, laughed and didn't miss a thing.

Men use brute force to load animals onto the Dun Aengus *to be taken to Aran Island. (Note donkey in background saying nothing, but taking it all in.)*

to another in very little time he could distinguish one from another. They used to say that he would early on have identified the beast most likely to lead the others astray by jumping a ditch or going down the wrong lane. He'd keep a close eye on that one. Sometimes they drove through the night. This is how Colum imagined it was at night for the drover:

> *I hear in the darkness*
> *Their slipping and breathing.*
> *I name them the bye-ways*
> *They're to pass without heeding.*

Like all other jobs there was probably a variety of people involved in it but, in general, people considered drovers to be quiet contented men, with animal instinct as well as human intelligence.

The drovers were the exceptions as far as such quietness was concerned, for most people at the fair were loud and agitated. Under the surface of excitement and business it always felt as if violence was lurking – a violence that could erupt at any moment. People seemed to be waiting for a reason to give vent to anger. This was unusual in a time when there was generally little antagonism in life but the fairs did bring out a certain wildness in people. Perhaps it was bravado; the fair marked some kind of climax – the seller was putting the fruit of his labour on public display, the buyer was displaying his expertise in spotting a good beast. Although I did love outings, I never tried too hard to get going to the fair. Fairs fascinated and frightened me in equal measure. I tried to stay near my father but he too could be carried away by the occasion and became less predictable than usual. The place would be full of tinkers, too, and they looked very wild. It seems to me, on reflection, that people came to fairs to fight. And of course everyone had a stick, a blackthorn stick; if the fight did break out it would be nasty.

At the fair itself, people with stock to sell stayed with their animals

The lesser Aran Islands had no harbours. Men had to row out in currachs to exchange their goods.

City folk knew nothing of fairs – they sold birds in cages.

and the prospective buyers walked around looking at what was on offer. Sellers and buyers surveyed each other and there was a good bit of animosity in that surveying. They circled each other like boxers in a ring before a fight. The animals, too, added to this atmosphere of impending danger; their eyes took on a glassy, blinded-by-fright look. They were unused to crowds of people and, I think, the hard surface under hoof made them feel unsure of foot. A step in any direction could become a slip, and then the farmer would roar, interpreting it as an attempted escape. This only compounded things. The disturbed cattle often put their heads on the back of the beast beside them, in an almost childlike search for comfort and consolation. The one whose back was used in this manner would itself already be under pressure and would shake it off with a shudder of fright that rippled through the whole herd.

Besides the farmers, drovers, tinkers and excited and frightened children, there were the cattle dealers who considered themselves to be gentlemen and thus a station or two above everyone else. They wore good clothes and they nearly always had mackintoshes – not the light type that tourists wear nowadays but real heavy rubbery stuff covered with off-white material. The mackintoshes had flaps and belts to be fastened and opened in different combinations depending on the weather conditions. And these men had an all-knowing smile on their faces. They wore either brown leather boots or good Wellingtons. Whatever they wore on their feet always looked as if they had been buffed and polished that very morning, and they had a way of keeping them cleaner than anyone else the entire day. They kept themselves a bit different from other fellows and they didn't appear to be anxious about the price they might get for their animals. They sauntered around confidently, keeping their boots clean. They had money in their pockets and they would take up whatever

Long before Female Lib tinker women looked and acted free.

A man of substance and importance always stood out at a fair. Here, in Killarney we see a pair of men one would be inclined to take notice of.

remained unsold at the end of the day. They could afford to hold on until better times. They were the ones who hired the quiet drovers to drive their stock. Cattle dealers wouldn't be bothered with such lowly work; they were entrepreneurs. They were among the first to have cars, along with doctors, priests and solicitors.

Doing a deal took a lot of psychology. It also called for a cool head but, at a fair, few people were cool. The times I saw it all, it made me very uneasy. Voices were raised and eyes flashed. People slapped animals on the back with bare hands. That itself made a very loud noise, but it was also backed up with a 'YUPP OUD THAT – YUP!' The already stressed beasts seemed to be driven by fear, strangeness and noise; they sought escape in every direction. The owner tried to prevent the escape, often with a strong blow of the blackthorn stick. This caused more commotion, more anger and more shouting.

When a buyer and seller came close to agreement on a deal they tended to shout even louder. Fury and excitement seemed to possess them. Someone nearby might nose in to seal the deal. The intermediary would attempt physically to draw the hands of the seller and buyer together, but if they didn't agree to the price they would not shake, no matter how much pressure was put on them. If they did agree they would spit into their hands, often two or three times, and then slap each other's open palm with another shout, 'DONE – THE DEAL IS DONE!' And then they went to the pub.

Some towns in Ireland depended on fair day for the bulk of their business. There were very few restaurants, or eating houses as they were called in those days. What there was depended on the farmers, jobbers, dealers and quiet drovers and the large amounts they ate on fair days. Spuds – as usual – would be the main ingredient of the meal, but there would be small mountains of vegetables on the plate, too – cabbage and turnips – and the inevitable bacon. Sometimes the bacon still had the skin on it and often times the skin still had the bristle. People used to call it 'hairy bacon'. The eating was as audible

Cabbages – definitely not imported and long before EU regulations about hygiene. This picture was taken in Moore Street in Dublin in the 50s.

Nothing like a good day out. Festive air at Courtmacsherry Regatta in 1953. There are swinging boats erected by the river and a traditional tinker's caravan by the side of the road.

as it was visible. They lashed into the food with a vengeance. They swallowed down large glasses of milk and didn't wait for it to settle before chasing it with forkfuls of potatoes. You'd even hear their boots on the floor; such would be their appetites from being on the road so early in the morning they couldn't stay still. They pawed the ground as they ate. Their boots, and even their clothes, would be all dung. They made the place awful dirty.

Not long ago, I was talking to a woman who used to run an eating house in Claremorris, County Mayo, at about the time we are talking of. She said it took forever to clean the place after fair day. It wasn't just the inside. First of all, you had to start on the street and get all the dung off the outside walls. The animals were so frightened and worked up that they urinated and defecated twice as much as usual. The woman believed that even the texture of the dung was different than that on the farm. Also the place would be so full with animals that many of them would be forced up against the buildings, and, as well as the dung, their hair had to be removed from the wall the days after the fair. Then the streets had to be washed down before you even started on the inside of the place.

The pubs did great business on fair days. When a deal was done it had to be sealed by 'drinking on it'. That could take time. It wasn't just 'a drink'; it could be 'the rest of the day drinking'. The inside of the pub would be steamy with human heat. Until they became drunk enough not to care, the post trauma of bargaining hung about the men and the place. They didn't stand still, they shuffled about the floor. People spilt drink, the shufflers spread what was spilt around until the whole place was awash with porter.

My first experience with the dangers of mixing drinks came in such a place and on such an occasion. I must have been about seven. My father had bought or sold and I went with him and the other man to drink on it. I wasn't asked what I was having I was given lemonade – red lemonade. Like the jelly, all lemonade in Ireland was red at that time. To this day Ireland is the only place in the world where I have seen red lemonade. I drank it down fairly fast, savouring the effervescence and then holding on to my empty glass. No one took any notice of me way down below them all. My father was very tall, and I only came just above his knee. I occupied a world of Wellington boots and sloppy floors and I had an empty lemonade glass in my hand. I tried to escape from this sad place by looking up. It wasn't easy. It was full and you could only get a slanted view of what was up there.

There was a poster on the wall advertising 'Club Orange'.

I was fascinated.

The poster was sophisticated. It depicted a very good-looking mother and father. They were all smiles and they had two children who were smiling, too. All four of them were drinking this Club Orange. They were so happy looking. I began to think that what was missing from my world was Club Orange. The boy in the poster had perfect teeth, shiny hair and he was bursting with happiness. I thought, 'its easy for you hanging up there in a glossy poster with not a spot of cow dung anywhere and drinking your Club Orange. But what have I got? An empty lemonade glass, a floor swimming in porter, loud noise and a bad smell and not a single soul taking a bit of notice of me.'

I decided to assert myself.

At the Galway Races this boy runs a temporary casino. He awaits punters to put their money on the table for a game of Crown and Anchor.

Before pigs started to fly they went by automobile to the pig fair in Athlone Co. Westmeath. Horses and donkeys were worried by this move towards automation.

I pulled at the hem of my father's coat. He took no notice. I pulled again.

'What do you want, child?'

'Daddy, I want Club Orange.'

Well, you'd think I had asked for champagne. 'Club Orange?' he exclaimed, with eyes open wide. His drinking companions were amazed, too. In the Irish language the addition of 'een' to a word gives the diminutive what is talked about – it is the equivalent of 'little' in English. Officially that is what it is, but, in reality, it carries subtle connotations. It can infer meanness, or a falling short of some target aimed at. It was often used derogatorily as well. Above the other comments about my request I heard this one – 'Well, isn't he the right little maneen with his "Club Orange"?'

It hurt.

However, one of them must have been an advanced thinker because, among spurts of saliva and laughter, he roared magnanimously, 'If it is

Club Orange the man wants 'tis Club Orange he will get.' Then he slapped a scatter of coins on the counter. I expected it was in excess of the cost, but I couldn't be sure because the counter was well above my eye level.

The drink arrived. I sipped and savoured. It was good. There were still bits of the orange in the drink and I flushed this through my teeth. Nice. I began to feel better – and more adventurous. I thought I should speak up more often and get what I wanted out of life. I was examining the panelling on the counter. I looked up and wondered what the top of that counter might be like. I was visualizing. I thought it had to be better than the floor I was standing on. I thought maybe it was nice and shiny. There was still a lot of Club Orange left in my glass. I would put my glass on that nice shiny counter and save myself the trouble of holding on to it. I reached up. I surprised myself with how big I really was. I had no trouble in getting the glass on to the counter. I couldn't see what I was doing but I had it up there.

Club Orange was still a designer drink in the Cork of 1953; it didn't appear on common posters. Most people were still drinking Paddy Whiskey and Ovaltine.

I told myself I hadn't been achieving my full potential in life – I told myself I should be stretching myself, expanding my boundaries. Then I told myself that my glass was far from safe on the edge of that counter up there among all those rough men who had little regard for the finer things in life – drinking black porter when they could be having Club Orange. I decided to push it in a bit.

I did.

I had anticipated that the counter would be about two feet deep. That's how deep other shop counters were; I knew, because I had often sat on them while my mother

TOP:
Aran sweaters, shawls and tweeds were the common dress of boys and girls. Now they wouldn't be found dead in them – strictly for the tourists.

ABOVE:
Tinkers caravan and horses at Fishmarket Quay, Galway.

did her shopping. Very gently I pushed the glass further in on the counter, guided by touch only. Inch by inch I got it out of danger. I was just about satisfied with where it was when it vanished from my feeling fingers.

Crash!

That's how I discovered pub counters were but eight inches deep.

'Jaysus!' my father scolded, 'look what you're after doing now.' He gave me a bit of a swipe with his hand. It only barely brushed me but the whole new world I had just built up for myself came crashing down around my ears. I cried. Down there among the Wellingtons

I became aware that the glossy world of advertising had little to do with reality. With a lonesome look up at that happy family I thought, what a chasm there is between their world and mine. They'd never know the reality of fair days in Ireland.

The going home was an awful scattering, too. They'd be saying the goodbyes for ages and slapping each other on the back all over again, saying what 'dacent' men they were. 'Twould take them half an hour to get out of the pub and another half to find the horse and cart. The horse would know they were drunk and he would be as scared as me – more I think. He'd get very skittish. He'd be tossing his mane and whinnying a bit. Sometimes the drunk men drove the horses extra fast and that really scared them. Their step would go all out of rhythm and they could even fall. I remember seeing some men wild with the drink standing up on the cart with the reins in their hands, shaking it to make the horse go faster and shouting more YUPP OUD THATs.

With the men coming home drunk from the fair the donkey came into his own again. It didn't disturb him but he didn't approve either; you'd know that. He'd be full of disdain for the drunkards but he did not let it upset him, nor his dignity, nor his pace. They could do or say what they liked: the donkey took no notice of drunk men or women's antics. He just went home at a speed and in a direction he decided.

Friends. There's room on my horse for two.

People knew that about donkeys so they wouldn't even take the reins in their hands if they were drunk. They'd somehow roll themselves into the cart and make some sort of a mumbling noise to the effect they were ready. But the donkey didn't even take notice of that. He wouldn't take a drunk's word for anything. He'd wait until he himself was satisfied that his human cargo was safely on board. Then he would soberly and surely amble home. It was fairly common to see drunks asleep going home on donkey and carts. It never worried anyone to see that; we all knew they were in safe hoofs.

There were a few major fairs that were held just annually. These

OVERLEAF:
'Bowls' was a Sunday Sport. It was played along the road with an iron ball. It was also a gauge of distance – 'a bowly down the road' meant you were the distance a good man might throw the ball from your destination.

were half-festival, half-fair. The mother of all these annual fairs was Puck Fair, held in the small County Kerry town of Killorglin – not too far from Killarney. This fair lasted three days: 11–13 August inclusive. No matter what day of the week the dates fall on, that is when the fair is held. They tried to change it once to coincide with weekend and something strange happened – a sort of curse, a result of changing the dates – so they reverted to the 11th, 12th and 13th, no matter what days they were. Puck Fair is still held but it is a mere ghost of what it used to be. Tourist now flock to the place and they think what they are seeing is as it always was. That is seldom the case with such things.

OPPOSITE:
In case of doubt this is Puck
Bar, Killorglin Co. Kerry
and Guinness is good for you.

Killorglin has a fine range of mountains behind it. Local men scoured these mountains for the most handsome puck goat that could be found. An all-white one was preferred. People used to have an eye out in advance, and be saying where the best-looking goats were. Goats are very beautiful beasts. The flow of hair of a good one can look like W. B. Yeats' 'The Cloths of Heaven'. The horns are lofty and of course the beard! It is that that really sets them apart from other animals. They have that lovely arty flow to them – especially in the wind the beard looks great. They look wise. I always think the best goats look like Ho Chi Minh.

Regal.

His little bit of a beard also had that twist to it.

Well, the goat that was picked was brought into town and crowned. He may have been robed, too, but that depended on how well dressed by nature he already was. If he had a great shiny coat he'd only wear the crown, but if there were any blemish in it they'd customise a costume for him. Thus, designer dressed, he was elevated on a platform forty feet high. He reigned for three days. 'King Puck' – Ireland's only king. That was what gave the fair its name: Puck Fair.

It was a real fair as well as a festival. Animals were bought and sold, especially horses and donkeys, but there was a lot more to it than that. There were tinkers and traders, jobbers and tricksters and you'd

King Puck – with all the dignity and disdain of any monarch worth his crown.

Hardy men with caps wearing their best and carrying their bundle waiting to be hired at a fair in Co. Galway.

never hear singers like you'd hear at Puck Fair. You'd have bad ones, too, of course, crowing away after a few pints, but no one took much notice of those. They'd let them wear themselves out. They'd eventually do that after endless ragged verses of 'come all yes'.

Then, when the real singers started, you could hear a pin drop.

That was one of the things about Puck: no matter how drunk they were a silence descended as soon as a good singer started up. Sometimes you'd hear an unaccompanied voice with a clarity that could pierce the air and strike the hills around. Another time a balladeer would bring tears to the eyes, and then the spell would be broken by some rascal with a bawdy song bringing back the laughter.

Even more than at the normal fairs there was a great tolerance for drink at Puck Fair. I once heard a woman describe her husband as 'a good man that never drank bar Puck'. And a man could sleep it off in any corner without fear of being mocked or robbed.

The three days of the fair were called Gathering Day, Fair Day and Scattering Day. During this time the town's population would increase from one thousand five hundred to fifty thousand people. They say it's not near that now: 'Aw, nathin' like it used to be.'

In olden times the hiring for the harvest was done at Puck. Hardy boys and men lined up along the street waiting to be hired. Servant girls, too, with their mothers, stood in groups looking for to be asked to do a job. There were weavers and spinners, coopers and basket makers, cobblers, tinsmiths, carpenters, animal castraters and poteen sellers. It is 'nathin' like it used to be' but still it stands as a marker from which time is counted. A story goes that one of the 'Paddies' working in the buildings in London in the sixties was complaining to another about how long it was since he'd been home. The friend asked: 'How long exactly would it be?' 'Come this Puck, it'll be three Pucks,' answered he.

*

Eamon de Valera (1882–1975) was an almost mythical figure in Irish history. He had a very romantic view of how he envisioned the people of this island living in a free republic. Despite the fact he was born in Manhattan, New York (the son of a woman from County Limerick and a Spanish sugar trader), he became Ireland's first Taoiseach, serving six consecutive terms from 1937 to 1954. The Irish Constitution was adopted by his government. Most people believe he was its main author and it may well be the case because it reflects his dream of the

De Valera laying the foundation stone of City Hall in Cork.

way life should be. It talks about 'comely maidens dancing at the cross-roads'. If Puck was the mother of all fairs in Ireland, the Rose of Tralee could be called, in de Valera's words, the 'comely maiden' of all festivals held in the country. Few people nowadays give a thought to its origins.

In the 1840s William Pembroke Mulchinock and Mary O'Connor would have spoken almost a different language, such was the difference in their social rank. Though they were both born in the town, they came from completely different backgrounds. He was from the big house: West Villa; Mary was from Brogue Lane, so-called because so many cobblers lived there. Mary's father was one of them.

William did not work. He was one of the three Mulchinock sons: William Pembroke, Henry and Edward. Their family owned not only their own huge house but much of the town as well. William was a dreamer and a poet and the family worried about him. They were very proud of Edward; he was the most likely son to carry on the good family name. They had little hope for William. Henry understood him and indulged him. He read his poetry and encouraged his brother.

But then Henry died. William was devastated. He wrote:

For him of the fair young brow I weep,
Who takes in the churchyard now his sleep;
For he was the star above Sun-bright,
Who tinged with the light of love My night.

These were not to be his most famous lines, however. After his brother's death William wandered aimlessly around Ireland, living near rivers, writing poetry and dreaming melancholically.

Mary O'Connor was a beauty. Her hair long and dark, her eyes bright, large, lustrous and brown. At seventeen she was taken on as kitchen maid in West Villa. She became a favourite among the large staff of chambermaids, groomsmen, gardeners and gamekeepers. They say the kitchen swelled with laughter and became a gathering place for all who wanted to hear and see her pleasantness. But she wasn't long in the kitchen. Maria Mulchinock quickly recognised in Mary the qualities that would make her a perfect nanny for her children. She was a gifted storyteller and the children loved her.

One day, sitting by the well, she had them gathered around her when their wandering Uncle William returned. They raced into his arms screaming and jumping and were surprised that he didn't lavish them with kisses and attention, as was his wont. Then they saw his eyes. He was transfixed by the beauty of Mary O'Connor. It was the first time he had seen her. They saw an unusual shyness come over her and they saw her look away.

They saw her blush.

It was love at first sight. But there was a problem. And what a problem! He was rich and Protestant she was a pauper papist. It could never come to anything. They went to dances at crossroads and danced 'up and down the platform' and people said what a shame it was that they couldn't marry. That they were able to do this is itself amazing. In those times, the gentry class wouldn't be seen dead with a poor working papist, never mind attending common goings-on with them. Dancing at crossroads! Definitely beneath the dignity of anyone from a manor house. But William did go to the dances and, in the end, didn't he ask her to marry him? She said nothing would make her happier but it couldn't be.

William went home and brooded and moped and doodled.

Then, one evening, he and Mary went strolling arm in arm along the stream and past the well to a stile. The sun was setting and the valley was hushed. William was a true romantic and he had picked his spot. He lifted her in his two hands and swung her up to sit on the stile and he sang to her the words of the song he had composed for her:

Playing the melodeon flute and fiddle in a Dungarvan pub. There was no television or radio so entertainment was live. Good musicians were the centre of attention and admiration. Everything went quiet when they started to play; men even suspended supping their pint – for a little while.

The pale moon was rising above the green mountains,
The sun was declining beneath the blue sea;
When I strayed with my love to the pure crystal fountain,
That stands by the beautiful Vale of Tralee.

She was lovely and fair as the rose of the summer,
Yet 'twas not her beauty alone that won me;
Oh no, 'twas the truth in her eyes ever dawning,
That made me love Mary, the Rose of Tralee.

The cool shades of evening their mantle were spreading,
And Mary all smiling was listening to me;
The moon through the valley her pale rays were shedding,
When I won the heart of the Rose of Tralee.

She loved the song but it scared her, too. Her family woes had been foretold in music before. It haunted them. The night her grandfather died ghostly music filled the air and they say that when his father before him died the same thing happened.

'Nonsense!' said William 'Will you marry me?'

She promised him an answer the next evening.

At that time there was a contentious election campaign going on among much political unrest in Ireland. The day after William sang his song to Mary there was a marching demonstration. A scuffle broke out. William, as leader of a group of men, was held responsible for the injuries sustained by a man called Leggett.

That night he met Mary. He didn't ask her anymore if she would marry him. He just opened a red velvet box, took out a diamond ring and slipped it on her finger. They were in an embrace when a messenger rushed on the scene. He waited until they stood apart before he gravely announced: 'Leggett is dead – you are wanted for murder.' Then he took from his purse a hundred gold sovereigns and, giving them to William, he said: 'I am to tell you to go to Barrow Harbour, there is a wine ship leaving there tonight.'

William found his way to India where he worked as a war correspondent. It was 1843 and the British were doing rather badly. One evening, William recognised among the dead the body of a fellow Tralee man, Lt. Collis. He requested to be allowed to take possession of Collis's belongings so that he could see they were safely returned to the dead man's family. The commander, who was to make a decision on this request, was called 'Old Gough'. He called in William and got from him his whole story. 'Old Gough' was a Limerick man himself and used his influence to help clear William's name and open the way for him to return, without threat, to his native town.

William got off the stagecoach outside The King's Arms, just a bit up the road from Brogue Lane. He went inside and ordered a cognac

before stepping down the street to see his Mary again. The landlord asked him the purpose of his trip and William answered: 'I have come back to marry the girl whose memory has sustained me through six years of heat and hardship in India.' The innkeeper was impressed. He said: 'It must be true love indeed if it has endured for such a time, but now you will excuse me, sir, I'll have to pull across the curtains for a few moments as there is a funeral coming down the street.' He did so and then the two of them looked through a crack in the drapes as the mourners passed. 'Who is it that is dead?' asked William.

'A young and beautiful girl,' the landlord said.

William heard ghostly music. 'And what may the name of the beautiful girl be?' he managed.

'Mary. She was so beautiful they called her the Rose of Tralee.'

William himself died at the age of forty-four. He found solace in alcohol. Before he died he added another verse to his love song:

In the far fields of India, 'mid wars dreadful thunders,
Her voice was a solace and comfort to me,
But the chill hand of death has now rent us asunder,
I'm lonely tonight for the Rose of Tralee.

Well harnessed horse and aproned driver carrying a load of stone building blocks along the quay in Limerick.

CHAPTER FOUR

'A Monk Swimmin''

'Blessed art thou amongst women' was commonly interpreted as being about 'a monk swimmin''. That seemed
reasonable enough; monks fell into the context of holy
things like prayer, and the 'swimmin'' could be something
to do with Jesus and baptizing John in the river.

It is hard for non-Irish people to understand how intrinsic Roman Catholicism was to the people, and indeed the land. It is as much a part of Ireland and the Irish people as the green fields and misty mountains, the fair skin and the freckled faces. It came with the talk, the laughter and the superstition and the stubbornness. There is some point in animal evolution where something, developed as a habit of survival, goes into the genes and is thereafter inherited by the offspring of the species. This is how Catholicism was for us, the Irish – it was in our very bones.

As has been said elsewhere – and it is crucial to the time-span of this book – things did not change much in Ireland from the mid-19th to the mid-20th century. There was little outside influence. Many people emigrated but they did not return. No influence was imported. There was no TV, and what radios there were were constantly tuned to 'Athlone' – the Irish radio station. In those times – up to the mid-fifties – I don't think the radios that existed were capable of getting much other than a crackle from 'foreign stations'. As well as that we were somewhat allergic to outside influence, mostly because such influences would be 'non-Catholic'. What had to be preserved above all else was our particular brand of fundamental faith.

As well as being in the marrow of our bones, Catholicism was in our hearts, in our hands and even on our doorways.

And it did endure for a long long time. When religious practice (of any denomination) was on the decline in the rest of the Western world, there was no hint of movement in Ireland. Even in the trendy sixties when other countries, especially England, just across the water, started to swing, we held steady. The girls put on their mini-skirts and the boys grew their hair to match the Beatles' but, as far as religious practice went, we held a steady course. The pill liberated sexual practices in other countries, in the USA and in Europe, but not in Ireland. There was no contraception here. The Catholic Church said it was not to be and the Irish people followed that dictate.

Even in the 1970s and 1980s, when all else was changing rapidly, our allegiance to and belief in Catholicism was barely dented.

When the change did come, it was rapid and devastating.

If you ask anyone in Ireland what the catalyst for the eventual change was, they will tell you, 'Casey of course'.

The *Irish Times* came on a story in February 1992 that it wanted to

Assembly of powerful people always showed up the prejudice that existed against women holding public office. DeValera, seen here addressing politicians, firmly believed a woman's place was in the home.

publish but dared not. It was about an Irish bishop and an American girl, Annie Murphy. The bishop was supposed to have fathered a son by the girl eighteen years earlier. It took the prestigious paper three months of research before it made the decision to go ahead. It had to be sure of its facts. The risk was great. Such was the strength of the Catholic Church in Ireland that publishing anything damaging to it could be the end of the newspaper. But by 7 May of that year it was sure. The paper published and Ireland was never the same again. The story that follows is no mere salacious gossip for, in terms of the effect it had on people's religious beliefs, it shook Ireland to the core. Eamon Casey was Bishop of Kerry first, and later Galway. He was a popular man beloved by the media. He was known to live the good life; he drove fast cars, dined at fine restaurants and liked to take a few drinks. He appeared on *The Late Late Show* (the top chat show on Radio Telefish Eireann) many times. The host of that show, Gay Byrne, fairly brimmed with mirth and patronage when His Grace the Bishop favoured his programme with his presence.

The bishop had a summerhouse overlooking the beautiful three-mile golden stretch of sand at Inch on the Dingle Peninsula, County Kerry. A friend in America had a young daughter, Annie, who was in something of a crisis. She needed counselling and advice. Could Casey help? 'Send her over,' he said. He would look after her.

He did.

He looked after her more than anyone ever anticipated. The long and the short of it is that she became pregnant. The bishop – fearful for his reputation – packed her off to Dublin where she gave birth to a boy. She ultimately returned to America and kept her son, and her secret, for eighteen years. The bishop never saw the baby but after Annie went home he did support her to the tune of $110,000 over the next eighteen years.

This, in a nutshell, was the story the paper published on that fateful day. The *Irish Times* was more interested in the source of the

Alfred O'Rahilly, fundamental Catholic apologist and President of University College Cork, wasn't a priest when this picture was taken. He became one later after his wife died. Here he is dining with Canon Thomas Duggan and Bishop Cornelius Lucey of Cork.

support money than the bishop's breach of celibacy. The cash had come from Church funds; Casey confessed to that. A short time afterwards he claimed the money was all refunded through 'contributions from several donors'.

Though the *Times'* prime concern was the money, it wasn't the public's. Their concern was about breaking the vow of celibacy. Ordinary people were devastated. Nothing remotely like this had ever happened before. In yesterday's Ireland, the Church had long been revered and trusted. It could be said that the Catholic Church was the backbone of Irish society. The opening sentence of our Constitution reads: 'In the Name of the Most Holy Trinity, from Whom is all authority and to Whom, as our final end, all actions both of men and States must be referred'. The Church hierarchy was as strong a force as the state. The Church was pivotal in Irish life. If people were in doubt about anything, it was the Church to which they turned. The Church was above human nature; it was infallible.

It is hard to estimate the impact of the scandal on Ireland. At first, people refused to believe what had happened – 'all lies', 'the paper won't refuse ink', 'aren't they always looking for something against the Church? – on'y lies, I'd say'.

But the truth refused to go away. Then reality took root. People started to blame her, Annie Murphy – 'brazen "wan", staying on her own in the bishop's house, leading him on, no doubt; a man isn't made of steel'. Many remained unforgiving of the lady.

Five years later, when the big novelty was gone out of the story, Annie Murphy was interviewed on the same TV programme and by the same host. Gay Byrne was not quite as effusive with Annie as he had been with Eamon. In fact, he didn't smile at her at all; he positively bristled.

Gay Byrne hosted his chat show for a quarter of a century. It was the longest running chat show in the world. He was an outstanding interviewer; he read an audience like a book. When he was writing the Constitution, de Valera said he had only to look into his heart to know what Irish people wanted; Gay Byrne had an even greater talent for reading the Irish public. The night he was interviewing Annie Murphy, though it was five years after we all became aware of what

OPPOSITE:
Kissing the Blarney Stone bestowed on one the gift of the gab; a smack at the bishop's ring before the match could swing the Almighty on side. The man in the suit has a 'fainne' (gold ring) in his lapel; that points him out as a fluent speaker of the Irish tongue. Dedication to the language and native games went hand in hand and was closely associated with and backed by the Church.

had happened, he knew the older generation of Irish people had not got over the shock of having the support pillar of the Church pulled from them. He felt it in his own heart, and it showed.

In the audience were relations of the bishop, elderly ladies sporting medals and crosses on chains and squeezing their handbags in disgust. Byrne remarked that he could see how Annie could be 'coquettish'.

He was in fact saying she tempted the bishop.

Peter, the offspring of the liaison, was also in the audience. Byrne talked to him. The smile came back. He remarked happily on how like his father he was and then he added, 'I hope you grow up to be half the man your father was.' By then the boy's father was in exile in South America; he had never once gone to see his son. He had used Church money, contributed by a dutiful congregation to be used for extending and beautifying their church, to keep the mother of his son quiet.

Cork women were great for the millinery. This opening of a church in Ballinlough in Co. Cork in 1938 provided them another photo opportunity to hold up their hatted heads.

Byrne, like a big number of older people in Ireland, could not admit the reality of the human fallibility of Irish clerics within the infallible Catholic Church. We – the ordinary Irish man and woman – were entrenched in our thinking about priests as all-powerful, never erring and gifted from God, with strength above ordinary human beings.

All-powerful ...

There is a story about an Irish priest and an open umbrella. A visiting American had left his umbrella behind in a farmhouse he had visited. The people of the house were intrigued by the instrument. They had never seen one before. After fiddling around with it for a long time they got the thing open, but they couldn't close it again. They were in the middle of a debate about how to get the thing outside the house. Someone suggested taking the door off the hinges, knocking some stones out of the wall and taking the 'up' umbrella out that way. Someone else said that was too much trouble; why not send for the priest?

They did, and he came.

Solemnity descends at the moment of Consecration at an open air High Mass.

There was no doubt but the priests had the power. They also had headgear and fine boots and they don't look too badly fed. This group is outside St. John's College in Waterford.

Of course, the priest was well used to umbrellas. While they were watching him, he, quick as a snake, closed the umbrella, swung it outside the door and opened it again, all in one motion. The family was full of wonder and the old lady of the house said, 'There is no doubt but the priests have the power.'

Most people who heard this story didn't like it, for it all but made fun of priest power. Everyone knew they were above the ordinary in all respects and it wasn't proper to joke about such things. Though we were young and childish and prepared to laugh at almost anything, jokes about the Church or the power of priests was beyond the scope of things to be made fun of. A bolt of lightning could come down and strike you dead for such blasphemy. Like Gay Byrne and Annie Murphy, we did not want to be associated with anything that underestimated the power of the Church and its priests.

Much later, some time in the eighties, only just before the Casey affair, a teaching colleague and I were talking about a recent tragedy that had occurred. A young boy had been electrocuted. He had been riding on top of a trailer-load of hay and he hit the overhead cables. My colleague agreed about the awfulness of the tragedy, but, she said, 'maybe there was a reason behind it'. Apparently the dead boy's father had gone against the priest; he had publicly disagreed with him. 'There's always bad luck following going against the priest,' she said. That was why the boy had been electrocuted, she thought. And that was an educated young woman's thinking on the cause of an accident in 1980s Ireland.

*

Priests were no ordinary people; they were selected by God to do His work on earth. Because He had picked them out as His special ones, we were to think of them differently from ordinary folk.

The selection process for the very special office of priesthood started very early. A priest would come around to National Schools and speak to the boys in fifth and sixth class, boys who would be reaching the end of their primary education. Many would be leaving school altogether and going to work on the farm with their fathers. Others, however, would be aspiring to secondary education. The priest would talk to them and explain what a 'vocation' was. A vocation was a calling from God to join the priesthood. You wouldn't hear this call. It wasn't like that: it was a spiritual message. God didn't shout out at you, nor did He appear saying, 'Your church needs you.' No! It was more subtle than that. He gave you the calling by equipping you in a certain way. The visiting priests told the boys how to judge if He were calling them. They were to ask themselves three questions. First, 'Have I got reasonable intelligence?'; second, 'Have I got good health?'; and finally, 'Have I the right intention?'

A newly ordained priest surrounded by his proud family.

That was the big one – 'Have I the right intention?'

The 'right intention' could be many things, like wanting to insure you went to Heaven, or helping pagans save their soul, or wanting to

A monk's cell at Mount Melleray

OPPOSITE:
The Cistercian Monks ran a guesthouse at Mount Melleray, Co. Waterford. Years ago it was a place where men who were fond of the drink went to dry out; nowadays people, men and women, use it as a peaceful place to reflect on life in a quiet and tranquil atmosphere under gentle guidance of the monks.

spread Christianity. Anything like that constituted a right intention, but wanting to become a priest because of the status or good life was not a right intention, and anyone going on for the Church with this intention was in for a land. It wasn't an easy life but it was a rewarding one. That is what the visiting priests said.

On the other hand, if a boy had all three signs of a vocation and failed to answer the calling, then some bad things lay in store for him. It wasn't spelt out but, with a wag of the finger and a knowing shake of the head, the licking of one's posterior by eternal flames was insinuated.

If a boy thought he had all these signs, the visiting priests offered free secondary education. They could so this because they had complete autonomy in running their schools. Religious orders had provided education before Irish independence; when independence came they continued to do so. A resources-scarce government was glad of this. It meant that it did not have to provide the service itself, but also it was in keeping with the ethos of the Independent Catholic Republic. The religious orders owned the schools (they still do in many cases), and they charged or did not charge fees as they saw fit. The offer of free education to boys who claimed to have a vocation wasn't made publicly. It was done discreetly. The priest would visit the parents of the boy deemed to have a vocation and he would tell them about the free education. It was inclined to firm things up. If the family was a strong farming one they might be expected to a contribute of some kind: a monetary one, perhaps, or, if they found this difficult, they could give 'spuds'. A bag of potatoes a few times a year was considered quite adequate.

Parents were very happy if their sons had a vocation. They were happy for many reasons. It was free education and a son off their hands; but most of all it was status. There was no greater assurance of social rank than having 'a priest in the family'. Those living off the land used to say that to make an impression in the farming community you had to have either 'a priest in the family or a pump in the yard'.

Brothers and nuns did the same canvassing operation in the National Schools but the status attached to having a nun or a Christian Brother in the family was very much a second best. I remember hearing the

Priests and nuns weren't allowed to visit their homes much; for nuns it might be once in seven years. Their coming was a big event that gave great joy to their families.

OPPOSITE:
Nuns made their own habits; for what they wore underneath they paid discreet visits to Sandy's of Dublin, tucked away in Cumberland Street.

mother of a priest comparing; she said you'd want at least two nuns to make up for one priest. A Christian Brother was about the same as a nun, maybe marginally higher. Masculinity counted.

Sometimes the recruiting was left until later, until the boys and girls were at secondary school. They would be approached in a similar way and asked to examine themselves to see if God was calling them to the religious life. The nun, priest or brother (Christian Brothers were commonly called brothers) called the prospective one into a private room and asked him or her about the vocation. Among themselves students used to joke about it; they called this interviewing 'popping the question'.

Once a boy or girl had made the decision to go on for the Church there was no way back. In theory there was, but not in reality. The disgrace attached to leaving the priesthood or the convent was great. It seldom happened, but in the few cases that it did there was terrible shame and embarrassment. I remember one case where a man did come out. His mother used to go to mass every day. Her house was a mile from the church. Every morning she turned right outside her own front door and, holding her head high, walked the mile to mass in the village. She went to communion every day with the head up, too. Then the son left the seminary and came home to her. He was not overly welcome. The lady stopped going to daily mass. Now, she went just on Sundays, but even on that day she no longer turned right outside her door. Instead she turned left and walked six miles with the head down to the nearest church in that direction. She could not face her neighbours after what had happened.

A few of those who did dare to come out often went to England; they fared better there. Over there they didn't understand; they weren't Irish Catholics. For those who stayed at home the derogatory stamp of 'spoilt priest' or 'ex-nun' was never erased. When it came to choosing a spouse it was a distinct handicap. The few who did leave seldom married; they were doomed to a life of whispered aspersions.

This group of postulants are of the Franciscan Missionaries of St. Joseph's, Blackrock, Cork. Girls with vocations were postulants for six months before becoming novices. They were finally professed nuns usually after two years altogether.

The majority who stayed on became priests, brothers and nuns. They taught school or went out to the Far East or to Africa 'on the missions'. Their task there was to convert pagans to Catholicism, so they could save their souls and go to Heaven. The faithful at home supported them enthusiastically.

In yesterday's Ireland, Irish people were very generous with what little they had. In every church and shop there were 'mission boxes', and in the schools, too. The priests who came around to the schools used these boxes as exhibits to promote the great job the priests and nuns were doing in converting the pagans.

There were different types of collection boxes, but the ones with the big emotive appeal were the 'black baby boxes'. These were rectangular with a little effigy of a black, kneeling, hand-joined child atop an aperture through which coins were dropped. These boxes were technically ingenious for their time. Underneath the slot for the coins was a lever that connected to the black child's head. When the coin was dropped in it tripped this lever and caused the head to bob up and down in a 'thank you' for the contribution. The boxes were masterpieces of marketing. In a pre-TV and radio-rare Ireland people, young people especially could not resist the nodding head. In schools where pennies were very scarce, children would line up with their coins and wait their turn to activate the nodding. It could be a slow process because, after dropping in a coin, a child was not likely to abandon his viewing position until every last echo of a nod had gone out of the 'black baby'.

Those religious who did not become missionaries – who stayed at home and became curates and later parish priests – commanded great respect and fear. Their power was almost limitless. They led their flocks in piety and no means were denied them in achieving the end of saving souls. The morality of the people of Ireland was their responsibility. Mortal human beings had to be saved from the eternal flames of Hell and sent on their way to eternal bliss in the company of Jesus Christ and His Mother Mary in Heaven.

Jesus and God were synonymous. God had sent down Ten Commandments on stone tablets from Heaven. To these Rome had added Six Precepts of the Church. It was only by following these ten plus six that one arrived at eternal salvation. Though the tablets were delivered long ago in some faraway place, most people believed these laws had a particular relevance to Ireland.

There was this sense that Ireland was the centre of the Catholic world and it was only from Ireland that others would get the message and be saved, too. Ireland was the interpretative centre of Catholicism. In National School we learned our prayers off by heart. We had no idea of what we were saying; we just said them:

These nuns are harvesting turf in 1936. The ones in the black veil are full nuns, the one in white is a novice.

Hail Mary full of grace,
The Lord is with thee,
Blessed art thou amongst women
And blessed is the fruit of thy womb Jesus.

'Blessed art thou amongst women' was commonly interpreted as being about 'a monk swimmin''. That seemed reasonable enough; monks fell into the context of holy things like prayer, and the 'swimmin'' could be something to do with Jesus and baptizing John in the river. I myself was a victim of dangerous curiosity. In innocence I asked our elderly lady teacher what 'womb' meant. Everything came to a halt. She stopped poking the fire, sat up, looked like she might faint, examined my face minutely for any hint of mischief and, finally, blinking and putting wisps of hair back, said, 'don't be asking questions about the prayers God taught us; they are to be said, that is it. Hail Mary ...'

In secondary school we had a subject called Religious Knowledge. When it came to the Albigensian Heresy I just kept my head down. I was not going to risk accusations of collusion by showing any interest in the affair. You'd know from the sound of it that it was indeed a nasty business; no need to know more. Curiosity could be a tool of the devil. I didn't need to ask anything about Luther. The name was close enough to Lucifer to know the two of them were involved in the same business. Calvin sounded more respectable, and he came from a posh country, but that was all a cover; he really was from the same stable as the other fellows. And, of course, Henry VIII was perversion personified. All he wanted was to satisfy his own desires of the flesh. He started Protestants so that he could marry a second wife and open wide the gates of Hell.

For the Irish it was a denominationally simple world. Other than Catholics there were only Protestants and pagans.

On Ash Wednesday, the first day of Lent, the priest made the sign of the cross on the forehead to remind people that 'thou art but ash and into ash thou shalt return.'

Protestants were beyond redemption. They were rich and would never listen to what the poorer Catholics had to say, so people didn't waste any effort trying to convert them. The churches they attended were places surrounded by superstition. It was deemed a sin to go inside one, but this was an unnecessary sanction – people were instinctively inclined to walk on the other side of the road from a Protestant church, anyway. One time, walking past a Protestant church on the way to our own, I heard an old man say to those walking with him, 'Wouldn't you think someone would tell them they are wasting their time?' The few Protestants around the country were a breed apart. They spoke with an English accent. There was little communion between the two faiths.

There were occasional, minor exceptions, to this lack of effort at saving the souls of Protestant neighbours. One of their members, a girl of five, joined a small school in County Waterford. This was a rare

More Cork women in hats. This is a Confirmation day at St. Finbar's South in Cork but the girls in their white veils and dresses in the background are completely upstaged by mothers and aunts with hats upon their heads.

OVERLEAF:
Processions were frequent. Good confirmation clothes could get an outing for such occasions. This one is for the blessing of a Grotto to the Blessed Virgin in St. Finbar's South, Cork in the late 30s.

Within the clergy costume varied: priests wore roman collars, De La Salle Brothers wore white 'bibs' and the bishop had a mitre and shiny cloak. This collection of holy men is at Newtown in Waterford.

occurrence. Protestants had their own schools, but for some reason this little girl didn't have access, so she joined the local Catholic school. After a few days her parents called on the Garda to report an attempt on their daughter's life. They claimed the other children had tried to drown her. The Garda investigated. Their findings were that the Catholic children had been trying to baptize the little girl. They had learnt in their catechism that 'outside the church there was no redemption'. They liked the girl and didn't want her to go to Hell, so they took her to a stream, the way Jesus had taken John. They had not contemplated total immersion. They merely intended sprinkling her with water and giving her an emergency baptism that would tide her over in the event of her passing on before a proper job could be done by a priest. However, fervour and zeal overcame them and the unfortunate child nearly lost her life in an attempt by innocent friends to save her soul.

In the hierarchy of importance the priest was the most powerful, respected and feared member of every community in Catholic Ireland. He said the mass, heard confessions, looked after the spiritual and temporal welfare of his flock. He also hired the teachers. National Schools were owned by the parish and managed by the priest. Secondary schools were owned by religious orders. Teachers got their qualifications from a state university or school of higher education (not Trinity College, Dublin: that was reserved for Protestants. It was a 'reserved sin' for a Catholic to attend Trinity). When qualified, the new teacher applied to the parish priest, or to the head of the religious institution who ran the school, for a job.

They selected meticulously. Applicants were asked about their private lives. It was assumed you went to mass at least once a week but you could be asked about other religious functions: did you do novenas? Who was your favourite saint? Did you pray much? Did you visit holy wells? And finally and most dangerously – did you 'keep company'?

Monks were different from ordinary priests. They wore simple habits, they didn't aspire to power but to personal enlightenment. The simple refectory here in Mt. Melleray Co Waterford reflects the simplicity of their lives.

Here we see nuns contemplating the finiteness of life at the wake of one of their members.

'Company keeping' was an occasion of sin. One shouldn't do it unless marriage was the intention. And if marriage was the intention, you couldn't be hanging around too long; you had to make up your mind and get on with the business of marrying because temptations could arise, that could lead to sin.

The big sin, of course, was sex.

In the Ten Commandments already mentioned, as well as 'sins of the flesh' they forbade things like eating meat on Friday, taking God's name in vain and backbiting, but they were only the lead-in. Talk about these minor bits and pieces like 'loving thy neighbour as thyself' – was just a way of getting at the really serious stuff without being too abrupt about it. You couldn't very well have sex at the top of the list. But, in truth, the sixth and ninth commandments were the hub of the whole business of staying out of Hell and getting into Heaven.

Sixth: Thou shalt not commit adultery.

Ninth: Thou shalt not covet thy neighbour's wife.

I doubt many people knew what 'adultery' or 'covet' meant and they didn't dare ask. Such questioning would be considered both metaphorically and anatomically below the belt, a belt south of which good Irish Catholics' curiosity was not to venture. A priest on the altar and the teacher in front of a class had considerable trouble in getting the message across. They dwelt on what was forbidden and spoke euphemistically about 'indecent conduct', 'immorality in thoughts, words, deeds', 'actions, that might lead to sins of impurity', 'sins of the flesh' and the curse of all soul savers – the 'bad thoughts'

All these things were to be avoided. One was advised not to think at all about the body; doing so could be an occasion of sin. If one's mind did wander in a corporeal direction then one should switch it back by uttering ejaculations. Highly recommended ones were, 'Jesus mercy Mary help' or 'Sacred heart of Jesus I place all my trust in Thee'; and a sure way back on track was to say, three times, 'Mary most pure protect me'.

The source of temptations was wide.

There were many occasions of sin but probably none so grievous as attendance at dances. These dances were held in some parish halls or, in earlier days, at the crossroads. The priest went, too, though he didn't dance. His function was to keep an eye on things. The lights were not allowed to be dimmed; the music was kept at a certain pace – not too fast and definitely not too slow. The priest would walk around the hall and give the hard eye to any man he saw holding his dance partner too close. He seldom had to do this because his presence was enough to dissuade any would-be impure actions, if not thoughts. After the dance he might take a scout around or out along the country road to see that the distance maintained in the bright public dance hall was not bridged in the comparative privacy of dark country ditches.

Dressage and the well dressed. Before tourists discovered how useful sidecars were for viewing scenery, the indigenous were using them for going to town for the messages and for the trips to mass on a Sunday.

The sound of the bells ringing from this church, Shandon, was of great significance to the people of the city of Cork. There was a song written about it.

There was a yearly 'mission', and this was a great opportunity for dealing with the impure thoughts and actions that led to impurity.

During the 'mission' everyone went to mass in the morning and went back to the church in the evening to listen to the priest's lecture. The mission was given by visiting priests. There would be two or three of them, members of religious orders. The Passionists were a favourite. They were an order of priests dedicated to contemplating the passion of Jesus Christ from the time of the Last Supper until he died on the cross. They wore sandals winter and summer; they had a black habit held around the middle by a cincture. From this hung a heart out of which grew a cross; the heart was scarred and bleeding. The message it conveyed was that 'impure thoughts and actions' wounded the heart of Jesus.

The mission was a great opportunity to hear it like it really was from a stranger. The local priest could hint at things and beat around the bush, but you didn't know exactly what you could or could not do. Strange priest could say things the local priest never would.

They talked about sex.

There were separate weeks for men and women, so the congregation was separated. This also led to greater openness on that very closed topic. Missionaries would tell you what you should and should not do. Some of them could be explicit enough so the mission also had an air of indulgence about it. It was better than the 'pictures' because one often felt guilty about things discovered through this medium. 'Pictures' were all made abroad, where people were not Catholic, so you could be committing a sin in finding things out through this medium. Being able to go to a church – definitely outside the sin zone – and to listen to a man of God talk about sex, was wonderful. It couldn't be sinful so prurience could be satisfied without endangering your immortal soul.

The mission was a time when people talked a bit more about these things. The women especially seemed to enjoy them greatly. You'd hear them openly hoping that he'd 'give them [the men] a hard time'. Women blamed men for sex and its contingent problems. They liked to give the impression they didn't like the thing at all. They only entered it unwillingly and under duress. Men were the perpetrators, women innocent and unwilling victims.

During the mission everyone was expected to go to confession at least once. This was an opportunity but it also posed a bit of a problem. If you had something that was bothering you, something you weren't sure was a sin or not, or, if it was a sin, what grade it was – mortal or venial – this was the time to clear it up with the stranger. People were shy about talking to their own priests about certain matters. The confession was supposed to be secret but still people were afraid the priest would know who they were. The mission priests wouldn't know you, and you'd never see them again. They were also considered more experienced. Hardened sinners only went to confession once a year at the time of the mission. Visiting missionaries were used to such cases; you could tell them nearly anything. These were the advantages. The problem was the amount of time he kept you in the confession box and the amount of penance

The temporary stalls that sold religious paraphernalia during the mission were a pure delight to children unaccustomed to the glitz of commerce.

he gave you. If you were inside a long time you'd get an awful looking-at when you came out. Sometimes these missionaries could be a bit loud and there was a great danger that the people outside might hear words that would give away the story of what you were talking about. The penance was also a problem. People would watch you when you came out to see how long you spent saying it. If it were long then they suspected you had much to tell. This was surmountable because the penance did not have to be said straight away; you could

go home and say it there. All in all, the mission was a good time to clear up any backlog. It was a time when many a young man and woman released great stress.

There was a kind of carnival atmosphere around the time of the mission, too. Extra candles would be lit in the church. There would be benediction in the evenings and incense smoke lingering in the air. But the biggest contribution to the celebratory atmosphere was made by the stalls outside the church. These were temporary structures of wooden framing covered with green canvas. They were a pure delight to a society unused to seeing the likes of what they had on offer. There would be all sorts of religious paraphernalia: rosary beads, scapulars, statues, medals, St Philomena's chord for tying around the waist, little crosses with a peephole in the middle through which you could see pictures of the crucifixion, relics, prayer books, crucifixes and pamphlets published by the Catholic Truth Society.

The cycle of life in the country centred on the religious calendar: Christmas, Lent, Easter and the 'mission'. Life was sheltered and cocooned, but it was secure. People felt safe within the particularly Irish brand of the Catholic faith. Though they might, secretly or with trusted friends, complain about particular priests or about the restrictions imposed by the Church, they trusted it implicitly. It was a safe port.

OPPOSITE:
The man who took this picture might not have even noticed the two loaves of bread to the left – priests probably would have ascribed spiritual inspiration from their appearance beside the poster. Family prayer was deemed to be the bread that sustained family life.

*

All that was shattered by the Casey affair. Many other Church scandals followed – most of them far more serious than the fathering of a son – but it was Casey's revelation that had the greatest impact. It showed the clergy up as being human after all – the same as the rest of us, capable of making mistakes. The myth of exceptional power and resistance to temptation was shattered.

Most important of all, Irish trust in the clergy vanished.

Society did an about turn. People began to ask themselves questions and look inside themselves for answers. They no longer turned to the Church for advice and counselling. The Church influence on state matters dwindled away. The numbers entering religious life tapered off. Today, having a 'priest in the family' is now as outmoded and meaningless as having 'a pump in the yard'.

CHAPTER FIVE

'Take Two Thorns from a Blackthorn Tree...'

'Fairies, now, are a different matter. I have never seen one but I wouldn't dare interfere with anything associated with them: the lone bush around which they are supposed to play or the *lioses*, the dwellings in which they are said to live. I am not alone in that. I don't think there is any Irish person who would. At least not one of my generation, or of the generations that went before me.'

Everyone has heard of the miniature Irish gentlemen called leprechauns, the little fellows with the green jackets and red caps, usually involved in the shoemaking trade. Americans love them. When I was a student I worked in a hotel down in Galway during the summer to earn the fees for the coming year. I had an American customer. She ate at my table day after day and, day after day, she became more and more depressed. She and her daughter, Mary-Lou (possibly not her actual name: time embellishes), had come all the way from Connecticut to see one of these little men. They had looked everywhere – under bushes, beside streams and in the bogs out in Connemara. Despite their constant vigilance, nothing. Then, with just a day to go before returning home, she and Mary-Lou dashed in to breakfast one morning. They were agog with excitement.

'We saw one,' Mary-Lou shouted.

The girl's mother had awakened very early; something had told her she should get up and look out of the window. She did, and there he was, sitting at the bottom of the garden, 'tap tap tapping on his li'le ol' shoe'. That's what the lady told me. Without ever leaving their bedrooms they had seen a leprechaun. Now they were ready to go home, 'mission accomplished'.

Well, I didn't believe them. I was all for them seeing what they had spent so much money wanting to see, but I thought they were probably still half-asleep. I thought it was the stars in their eyes they had seen and not a leprechaun. I didn't believe in leprechauns.

Fairies, now, are a different matter. I have never seen one but I wouldn't dare interfere with anything associated with them: the lone bush around which they are supposed to play or the lioses, the dwellings in which they are said to live. I am not alone in that. I don't think there is any Irish person who would. At least not one of my generation, or of the generations that went before me.

In the thirties there was great talk about transatlantic flights. One of the problems was the great distance to be covered and the inability of the aeroplanes to carry enough fuel for such distances. In 1934 the Irish government was well aware of Ireland's strategic position with respect to Europe and America. We were the last landfall before the New World; all Europe was to our back and the Atlantic Ocean

The Fairy Tree. Lone blackthorn bushes were reputed to be the centre of a fairy playground. This knurled specimen might have seen a thing or two.

swelled up in front of us. Ireland was the last point where planes could be topped up with fuel before heading out over the great ocean. There was business potential in the way the good Lord had placed our little island. The government decided we should have an airport. They said it could do awful well. Flying boats had made a few crossings of the Atlantic and the possibility of commercial transatlantic flights was becoming a reality. They decided to build.

Plans were drawn up. The drawings were brought to the location and stretched out on a desk, in an office overlooking the site. The men who were to do the digging were all lined up with their picks and shovels. They were shown the spot where the runway was to be and they were ordered to dig.

As one, they said 'No!'

They said they wouldn't dig out the foundations as the architects had drawn them. They said the plans would have to be changed and the runways would have to go in a different position.'

Why?

Because there was a *lios* in the path of the proposed runway and no one would touch it. They, like all Irish people, would not interfere with fairy dwellings. The consequences could be terrible.

The plans were changed; the *lios* was saved, the runway was put down in a different place and, so, the first Pan Am flight Boeing 314 landed safely on 28 June 1939.

These *lioses* can be seen more clearly from the air than from the ground. They are circular constructions. They are underground dwellings, but above ground you can see the circular humps. They are, for all the world, like waves of earth. Imagine dropping a stone in a pond and, from above, seeing the ripples spread out from where you dropped the stone; that is what a *lios* looks like, only the ripples are of earth rather than water.

*

When I was at boarding school in Mount Melleray in County Waterford, the man in charge of us was a Cistercian monk. He was an intelligent, curious man and he liked those in his care to be curious, too. If you were, he did all he could to satisfy that curiosity. In 1957, when the Soviets launched the first satellite, he told us what he could about it. Then, when he had exhausted his own knowledge, he called us at 5.30 a.m. to go outside and see it. I did. It emerged over the Knockmealdown Mountains like the star that guided the Wise Men who went to Bethlehem. It passed over our heads and disappeared into the horizon. I remember thinking how spooky it was. I had a feeling I was witnessing something that had great implications for the future of mankind.

My questions about fairies got an equally scientific response.

He took us on a walk one Sunday to see a lios. It was as I have described above, but, of course, being earthbound, we were not able to see the circular construction as clearly as one would from the air. However, this good and holy monk walked us all around its perimeter to get the feel of it. Then he showed us the entrance. It was very low and to go inside you had to crawl on your stomach. Inside it was like an igloo. Whoever used this must have been very tiny. At the time I was thirteen and small for my age, but inside I could not stand up. Our monk could not even get in through the opening and he wasn't very fat. He had brought candles and matches and we had a good

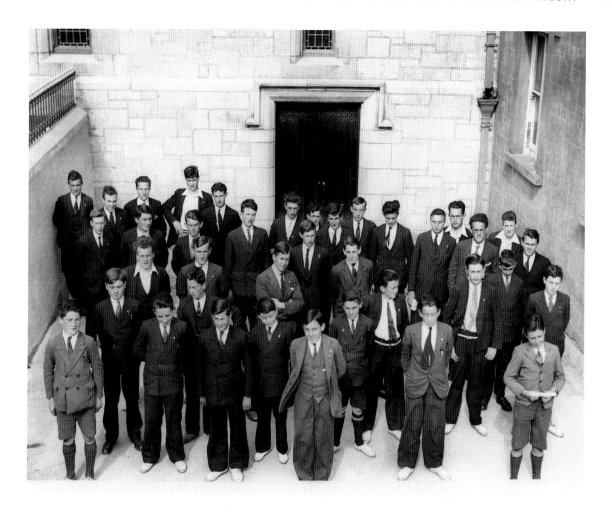

Students of Mount Melleray Seminary Co. Waterford all dressed up and hair slicked down for prize giving day in the early fifties.

look around inside. It was built hundreds, and maybe thousands, of years before the Soviets launched their satellite, but the inside of this edifice inspired a wonder similar to the silent satellite ploughing the morning sky.

Nobody was too sure what fairies were, how big they were, how real, or if they were forces for good or bad. You just didn't interfere with the places with which they were associated. As well as *lioses*, lone trees or bushes were often associated with fairies. People believed trees standing alone marked the meeting places of the 'little people'. Because of their power there was always an association between the fairies and religion. We were encouraged not to be afraid of them. But you often got the feeling that those doing the encouraging were not too convinced in what they were telling you. They sounded like they

Count John McCormack (right) with his wife Rose and children Cyril and Gwendolyn on a ship leaving America for Ireland in March 1924.

were afraid themselves, that they were just trying to persuade you they were not.

John McCormack (1884–1945) was Ireland's most famous tenor. Trained in Italy under Sabatini, he made his debut in London's Covent Garden in 1907. He was the youngest tenor ever to do so. You would expect one with such credentials to be best remembered for an aria from some opera, but Irish people associate him mostly with his wonderful rendering of a simple song about a fairy tree near a small village called Clogheen, in a beautiful mountainous spot of County Tipperary. McCormack said about his audiences: 'I give them the folksongs of my native land, which I hold to be the most beautiful of any music of this kind.'

The song that follows was composed by Temple Lane, the pen-name of Isabel Leslie, daughter of the Rev. Canon Leslie, who at one time ministered in St Mary's Protestant church in Clonmel. The words of this song go a long way to describe the spirit of Irish belief in fairies and their power:

The Fairy Tree

All night around the thorn tree, the little people play,
And men and women passing will turn their heads away.
They'll tell you dead men hung there, its black and bitter fruit,
To guard the buried treasure round which it twines its root.
They'll tell you Cromwell hung them, but that could never be,
He'd be in dread like others to touch the Fairy Tree.

But Katie Ryan who saw there in some sweet dream she had,
The Blessed Son of Mary and all his face was sad.
She dreamt she heard him say 'Why should they be afraid?'
When from a branch of thorn tree the crown I wore was made.
By moonlight round the thorn tree the little people play
And men and women passing will turn their heads away.
But if your hearts a child's heart and if your eyes are clean,
You'll never fear the thorn tree that grows beyond Clogheen.

Even more elusive than fairies were pishogues. I am reluctant to use the past tense because, even though I think young Irish people know or care little for them, it is hardly correct to think of such things as being no more. By their nature, if they have a past they have a present. Like 'luck': if it was, it is.

What pishogues (an anglicized version of the Irish 'piseoga') were or are is vague; even as a part of speech the word is hard to define. Certain actions were deemed to be pishogues, but beliefs also were. So, the word that is used to describe beliefs is also used to describe certain actions. If you said it was bad luck to come in and out of a house using the same door, someone would accuse you of believing in 'ol' pishogues'. Then I remember one time asking my grandmother what Kate, an old neighbouring woman, was doing bent over down at the end of a boggy field; she said with a bit of a tremble, 'come in out of that, child, and don't be looking at her, she's at the pishogues'.

A lot of pishogues surrounded cows and milk. If the cow wasn't inclined to give milk they believed someone had done pishogues. If the cream didn't turn into butter after you dashed it in the churn, that was pishogues, too; and if a woman was seen skimming the top of water from a pond on your land she was said to be doing pishogues, and it would have a bad effect on your cows. They wouldn't give much milk but her cows would. There was the idea that 'luck' was in limited supply and that you could take some of what was available for yourself at the expense of someone else. African witchcraft has the same basic idea of limited supply of good fortune; its exponents believe you cannot create good fortune, you can only divert it. You can only increase your store of good luck at someone else's expense.

The banshee was easy enough to define. Definitely a woman and, like all women, to be feared. She did an awful lot of wailing. I find it hard to believe I have never heard her myself, because, I feel, I can hear that terrible sound in my head. Such was the vividness with which those who did hear her described it to me – an awful wailing, crying and screeching.

The banshee followed certain families, usually families whose name started with 'O' or 'Mac'. When one of the members of such a family died, she cried. This cry could be heard by all of that clan, or a member of any other family whom the banshee cried for, too.

Once I met a sick man in Galway. He had cancer. He told me he had heard the banshee cry for himself. He said he knew he hadn't long to go. 'Going up the boreen to my own wee place last night, I heard her' is what he said to me. Later a neighbour told me that he saw Seaneen (that was the sick man's name) going home that same 'last night', and that he was 'three sheets to the wind'. The neighbour said, 'I don't know where he gets the strength from, but he was screeching like a banshee going up the boreen.'

My own uncle once frightened the life out of me running all around the farmyard one night in his long johns and shirt. This was nothing to do with the banshee but it had to do with a loud noise. The cock crowed during the night, a sign that someone in the house was going to die, so the uncle ran out to try to make him change his mind and save us all. I heard the commotion and jumped up to see

OPPOSITE:
The reputation the Blarney Stone has of giving one the gift of the gab was bestowed on it by none less a person than Queen Elizabeth I of England. A McCarthy from the locality had a way of getting concessions from her majesty. She was aware of her vulnerability to his charms and she said ' That man is full of the Blarney'. She went to her grave never knowing what she had done for Irish Tourism.

the bizarre scene out of the window. I went downstairs to meet my uncle coming in the door. He was dripping sweat and only half of it was from exertion; the rest was from raw fear. He told me not to worry; he said it would be all right, that he had stopped the cock in time, that he had saved us all.

'Anyway it could be worse,' he said.

He said if it was a hen that was crowing at night you might as well throw your hat at it, there was no reversing a hen crowing at night. A cock wasn't so bad if you got to him in time to stop him, but once a hen had crowed you couldn't change her mind.

The time of year had big implications for all these superstitions and there was no more auspicious time than May Day. Preternatural forces abounded on, and around, this day. In my own memory nothing was left out of the house on May Day. It was believed that anything going out took the luck with it. In olden times they didn't have matches; in many houses the fire was kept going all night. It was easy to keep a turf fire going. You just piled the ashes on it at night and removed them in the morning. Then, you added a few sods and in no time the fire was in full glow again. Sometimes neighbours came for a bit of 'gresha' (hot coals from the fire) if theirs had gone out overnight. Well, on May Day they wouldn't get it. Nothing could leave the house on that day. I heard that in County Galway they were afraid that the smoke going up the chimney could be spirited away by someone adept at pishogues. I heard it was believed that some women who did pishogues would stand a distance from a house that had smoke coming out of the chimney, and that by fanning their apron and backing into their own house they could coax the neighbour's smoke in after them. If this happened people believed such a woman stole all the luck and took it into her own house.

A lot of these beliefs surrounded dairy produce and certain animals.

Cows gave milk only after calving. If a neighbour's cow was in calf it was customary to give them a bottle of milk each day to keep them going until the cow had calved and they had there own. On the day before May Day two bottles would be given because no one gave anything away on May Day – especially anything to do with, cows, goats, milk or fire. And this tradition goes back a long time. In *Britannia* (1586) William Camden

tells us what a priest in Limerick called Good who 'about the yeere of our Lord 1566, taught school at Limerick' told him:

'They take her for a wicked woman and a witch what ever shee bee, that commeth to fetch fire from them on May-day (neither will they give any fire then, but unto a sicke body, and that with a curse): For because, they thinke the same woman will the next summer steale awaie all their butter. If they finde an hare amongst their heards of cattaile on the said May daie; they kill her, for, they suppose shee is some old trot, that would filch away their butter. They are of opinion that their butter if it bee stolen will soone after bee restored againe, in case they take away some of the thatch that hangeth over the doore of the house and cast it into the fire.'

Up to very recent times people associated hares with witches. Hares were especially feared. It was thought that a witch could turn herself into a hare for purposes of concealment. One popular childhood story concerned a man who saw a hare among his cattle on May morning. He gave chase and got close enough to the hare to inflict an injury on it, but the animal escaped. He followed the trail of blood and it led to a house where an old woman lay bleeding.

My own father used to hunt rabbits. He was very good at catching them and we were very good at eating them. He seldom caught a hare. One time he did. He immediately removed the scut (tail) and stuck it between two stones in a ditch. I asked him why and he said it was to bury the bad luck one might incur from killing a hare. When we got to the house he told my mother what he had done but that did not satisfy her; she said he could leave the hare outside, that it was not lucky to bring it into the house. She didn't like that he had caught one at all. I felt a bit uneasy about it, too. To this day I get a bit of a start when I see a hare.

There were many non-medical cures for ailments, too. Sties in the eye could be cured by taking two thorns from a hawthorn bush and pointing them away from the sty. Then, the thorns were thrown over the shoulder and soon the sties went away. For warts it was a snail you used. You got the snail and rubbed it to the wart. Then you found a hawthorn bush and stuck the snail to it. As the snail died and its body decayed so did the wart.

Many of these old cures seemed to work and nobody knows exactly why. It may be because people believed in them, it may be the placebo effect, but there could be other reasons, too.

In olden times if a child had whooping cough you walked the road until you met a man riding a white horse. You asked him what you should do with the child. If you followed his instructions exactly the child would get better. So people believed anyway.

When I first heard this story I thought, 'what a strange superstition'. I thought it was all old rubbish. Then, years later, travelling in Guatemala, in Central America, I came across a remote country place where lines of people were queuing up for nearly a mile. The place they were all waiting to see was most unimpressive. It was the smallest little farmyard you ever saw, with a few miserable looking hens dragging their wings along the ground they were so malnourished. The owner of the place was a potbellied sweaty man, who had his shirt off.

The cause of the sweat was the work he was doing.

The Kinsale cloaks these sellers of shamrock are wearing in Cork 1916 are probably commercial props; the fox furs and elegant costume of the buyers are not. Cork women were great for putting on the style. And who has the boy in the background got his eye on?

He was rocking a chair. In the chair was this thing which resembled a mannikin from a shop window. The 'statue' (though not exposed) was obviously male. He wore sunglasses – Ray-Bans they were. He had a cigarette holder, with a lighted cigarette in it, in his mouth and a black hat on his head. He had cowboy boots and a Spanish looking jacket and trousers on him. I discovered later that he was called Señor San Cimon (the statue – not the sweaty farmer). He is considered a very powerful saint in Guatemala.

This is what the people were lined up to see. When they reached him they huddled into him and muttered away all their troubles. They had offerings of rum, cigarettes and money. The potbellied man tilted the 'statue' back in the rocking chair, the pilgrims poured rum into the mouth, opened by the tilting, and put a new cigarette into the holder. They poked a few notes into his pocket and waited for whatever advice he had to give. I heard nothing but they seemed to. They walked away with a much lighter step and a relieved smile on their faces. Every now and then the sweaty farmer switched the notes from Señor San Cimon's pockets to his own. This seemed to make no dent in the belief of those lined up, nor did it seem to diminish their faith in the Señor.

It was in trying to work this out that I first got to understand the man on the white horse and the cure for whooping cough back in Ireland. Señor San Cimon was dressed up to look like a conquistador – one of the original Spanish settlers in Guatemala. For the humble peasants who gave him rum and cigarettes, he represented power from some strange, foreign land. By the time I saw him, the Spaniards had been in Guatemala for a number of centuries, but the native population continued in the belief passed down by their forefathers that the new settler from the Old World was very powerful and full of knowledge about how to solve problems and cure illnesses. And, of course, in older times the rum and cigarettes would have bought many favours from the new masters.

Faith, fear and fortune were fairly mixed. At St. Colmcille's Well, Ballycullen, Rathfarnham, Co. Dublin the girl in the foreground seems to have been dealt a poorer hand and clothes than those around her.

On Pattern Days people gathered at graveyards and crossroads. The stated purpose of such gatherings was to clean up the graves and do a bit of praying. That done there was the night long for singing and dancing. This is a Pattern Day in Lettermore, Co. Galway.

I think the old Irish tradition about a cure for the whooping cough had a similar origin. A man with the white horse would be no ordinary person. He would have to be of wealth and power to have such a steed. It could be, indeed, that doctors went around on such animals – a kind of ancient ambulance with harness bells instead of a siren.

What the Guatemalans and the Irish had in common was a belief in the power of people whom they considered superior. The white horse was a sort of symbol of superiority, as were the Ray-Bans and cowboy boots on Señor San Cimon. No matter that the 'shades' and cowboy boots were out of period – they still signified power. Superstitions may have ancient roots but modern bits and pieces are often added on.

Most of these beliefs and superstitions in Ireland, as in other places, had their origin in ancient times and were added to as other influences came into play. Saint Patrick was successful in his mission of converting Ireland from paganism to Christianity because he was, basically, a politician. He was a master at putting spin on things. He didn't believe in disturbing the natives too much. He built the new Christian practices around the old pagan customs.

He manipulated things.

He knew the Irish were a stubborn lot. Instead of trying to bulldoze them into the new habits, what he did was add bits and pieces to the old ones. It is clear, then, that the Irish were, and are, superstitious. They were always big on pilgrimages. In County Mayo people were doing pilgrimages to what is now called Croagh Patrick long before that good man ever came our way. Ancient kings, chieftains and druids walked along a road for days, a road that led to the top of the mountain. When Patrick found out this he did the same thing. He led his followers up into the mountain to pray, too. Only difference was when he got to the top he paid homage to his god, Jesus Christ; the druids and

The graves at Clonmacnoise go back a long way – no one knows exactly when the place started being used as a burial ground but it was before the tower at the right of the picture was built by the Normans in the twelfth century.

chieftains worshipped the sun. The Irish were ripe for the picking; they were superstitious and loved outings. We have changed a bit now, what with everyone having cars and things, but until thirty years ago, more or less, there was nothing to beat a pilgrimage to some holy place.

Croag Padraig was one of the favourite places and it's still going strong. Tourists come from all over the world now to climb to the top; maybe they are as much interested in the scenery as any spiritual benefits accruing to the trip, but in olden times it was undertaken as a punishment for sins. Old and young climbed to the top over stones and sometimes they did it in bare feet. It rains a lot in Mayo so it was not an easy journey. You'd see people bent over from exertion and the feet would be bloodied. But the faith was very strong. The exercise was good, too, and there was no doubt about the camaraderie that arose between people doing the pilgrimage. The best often comes out in human beings when they are united against the hardships of the elements

Another place of pilgrimage in Mayo was Knock. I shouldn't say 'was' for it still is. It very much 'is'. Hard to believe this harsh and stony place of winding roads can now be easily accessed by aircraft direct from New York, Boston, London and points east and west to the local airport. In my youth no one would believe that such a miracle could come about.

They say that 21 August 1879 was a bad weather day for the west of Ireland. It rained heavily. As night came down some people in the small village of Knock saw a light glow on the gable end of the local church. Then they saw it taking human shape. There was a lady in white. A man appeared at her right-hand side and then another on her left. The second man held a book open and appeared to be reading from it. His hand was held up as if he were trying to make a point, as if he were preaching. An altar appeared beside the preaching man and on this altar there was a lamb. Behind the lamb, a cross. A circle of angles hovered over the whole lot.

The scene was witnessed by twenty people on that wet August night more than one hundred and twenty years ago. They were a mixed group of various ages. The glow from the apparition was seen miles away. People heard about it. They started coming to Knock. The sick

and infirm came to pray. Some claimed cures – many said they found
the atmosphere inspiring, they said they found it peaceful and calm-
ing. The Church investigated the matter and deemed the account of
the witnesses to be 'trustworthy and satisfactory'. They said the
apparition was of Our Lady, St Joseph and John the Evangelist.

The numbers visiting the place grew.

With the motor car and improved roads, the traffic to the place
increased. Parish priests from all around the country started organis-
ing trips to the site of the apparition. People left their homes early in
the morning, travelled all day, and came home late at night from the
'Pilgrimage to Knock'. It became something that every woman was
expected to do. In fifties Ireland there wasn't such an onus on men to
pray. They did Croag Patrick all right, but Knock was more for the
women. I think the hardship of going up the mountain barefoot made
the mountain climb respectable for men; going to Knock by bus was
more for the women. 'Twas a bit like hanging out the washing or
pushing the pram – a woman's job.

When the women reached Knock, they prayed for their men. They
took raincoats and headscarves and a rug for around their knees on
the bus. They took flasks of tea and bread and butter wrapped in
newspaper. The better off might have sweet cake or apple tart. They
took bottles. Any neighbour who wasn't going that year would give
the woman who was a bottle to bring home the holy water. The priest
went with them. He and the driver would be the only men on the bus.
The priest would lead the rosary. They would say fifteen mysteries
(each of the divisions of the rosary corresponding to the 'mysteries of
redemption') on the way there and another fifteen on the way back.
It shortened the journey and increased the chances of having your
requests granted.

The greatest miracle of all accredited to Knock was the airport built
to service that remote place. There may have been divine intervention
but a very earthly man set the ball rolling.

*Praying women around a statue of Our Lady in Knock, Co. Mayo. Most of the praying
was left to the women; they seemed to be better at it. Going down on bended knee didn't
come so natural to the men, they were a bit shy.*

OPPOSITE:
The pilgrimage to Lough Derg took three days. Two nights were spent on the island. One night you were allowed sleep. The other night and two days were spent doing penance for sins, walking barefoot around stony beds dedicated to different Saints.

That man was Monsignor James Horan. He became parish priest of Knock in the 1970s. He was a man of ambition, foresight and business acumen. A friend of mine told of an acquaintance who went to confession to the Monsignor and came out owning a house: the Monsignor had sold it to him while he was forgiving him his sins. Horan had big plans for Knock. He wanted to put it on the international map. He wanted it to be as familiar to Catholics as Lourdes was. He was losing business to the French. Knock needed a spotlight on it. It needed a boost. It needed a personality. It needed someone really important to go there.

Lesser men might have thought of a national politician or a show-biz personality.

Not Horan. He got the Pope of Rome.

He pulled every string in ecclesiastical puppetry and came up with the top man: John Paul II. He came all the way from Rome on the Seven Hills to Knock – a small village in a remote corner of Ireland. He was there to mark the 100th anniversary of the apparition, in August 1979.

After the visit Horan said, 'with people like the Pope coming to Knock we can't be expecting them to be all day on the bus from Dublin'. He said Knock needed an airport. People laughed. It became a running joke. If something was extremely unlikely to occur they'd add 'like Knock airport' to the suggestion.

The Monsignor started to gather money. First he got a grant from the government and people said they were trying to placate Horan; they said they were looking for votes from Mayo. Then he organised visits from big shots with Irish ancestry in America, including the actress Grace Kelly (Princess Grace of Monaco) who bought the cottage her father had lived in for £7,800 and intended building a small holiday cottage on the site. He also made use of the Kennedy Irish connection to fundraise from the richest and most successful Irish Americans. The money poured in. Although he appeared frequently on TV and radio shows, still we kept on laughing at him and his idea about an airport in Knock in the middle of the bog. We said he was for the birds – we said nothing would ever fly into Knock – only snipe, and they would be reconnoitring for better pastures. But the laugh was on us. The airport was completed on schedule and on budget.

The first jumbo jet landed there in 1986, only seven years after Horan had first come up with the idea. (Ironically, the Monsignor died a few days after its opening ... on a pilgrimage to Lourdes.)

*

Lough Derg is in County Donegal. It is called St Patrick's Purgatory for the saint is supposed to have done punishment for his sins there on a little island on this lake. The only way to get to the island is by boat and the only way to get to that boat is by bus. Lough Derg is even more remote than Mayo. Also it requires more effort because the pilgrimage takes three days. In his poem, 'Lough Derg', the Inniskeen-born Patrick Kavanagh (1904–67) wrote: 'A Leitrim man / With a face as sad as a flooded hay-field, / Leaned in an angle of the walls with his rosary beads in his hands.' Pilgrims come from all over.

The form is to go across by boat and take off your shoes straight away. Then you start praying, going around 'stations'. There are 'beds', stony bits dedicated to various saints: Brigid, Brendan, Catherine, Columba, Davog and Molaise.

I 'did' the pilgrimage just once, more than forty years ago. There was a great feeling attached to the 'doing' Lough Derg. Even though I, personally, haven't been back, many tell me they still get that feeling today. You ate no food, only 'Loug Derg soup'. I was full of youth, enthusiasm and fervour but I also had the powerful appetite of youth and open air. The fasting didn't worry me because I had heard you could eat as much soup as you liked. Having been brought up on the stuff, I thought I would have no bother. The soup my mother made was full of vegetables and bits of rabbit meat; it was nutritious and filling. Too late I found out Lough Derg soup was different. It was in fact water from the lake spiced up with a little salt and pepper – nothing more. But I felt spiritually elevated after the visit.

You had a bed while there, but of the two nights you were only allowed to sleep one. The other night was spent in vigil. You spent the night walking around the 'stations' and 'beds' in bare feet. Every now and then you went into the church to get warm (it is very cold on Lough Derg all year round) but you were in danger of nodding off, so you quickly took to the rounds again. This was not altogether a free

choice. There were priests; if they saw you nodding off in the church they indicated with a wave of their walking sticks that one would be better off in God's open air. Outside they walked around 'helping' people do the pilgrimage 'properly'. They had unsubtle ways. I remember one couple holding on to each other as they picked careful steps through the sharp stones; the priest looked suspiciously at them. Then, I heard him thunder: 'Are you married?'

They weren't.

They were ordered to unlock the helping hands and struggled on separately.

There were less arduous ways of getting merit. In the forties and fifties in Dublin many 'courting couples' spent their time together going around to novenas. It was cheaper than the cinema and, they hoped, held long-term promise of a happy union when they could afford to get married. These novenas – devotions which consisted of services or prayers recited on nine consecutive days – were held all over the city. Thursday nights in St Michael the Archangel's, Fridays in St Benedict's, Mondays in St Jude's. But, of course, Tuesdays were reserved for St Anthony. Anyone who knew anything at all about Irish Catholicism knew that Tuesday night had to be reserved for that man. St Anthony was good at finding things, but you had to pay him to do so. Failure to fulfil a promise of payment for a service done mean that you didn't get any help the next time round. Merchant's Quay church on the Liffey in Dublin had a special box for collecting money owed to St Anthony for finding things.

In Aungier Street church in central Dublin there was a novena on Wednesday nights and it was nearly all women used to go there. The women tended to be over thirty and mostly they were country girls working in the city who were excluded from whatever system was in operation in their part of the country for finding a partner. The novena was to St Anne and finding a man for a woman was this saint's speciality. Dublin children had a skipping rhyme that went:

Oh! Holy St Anne
Send me a man
As fast as ever
You can can can

Devotion to prayer was quite incredible. It was hard to find anyone who didn't believe in the efficacy of pilgrimages and devotions. And it continued on until very recent times. In the eighties there was a great commotion about statues that were said to have moved. Many people claimed to have seen statues come to life and give messages about impending danger or unhappiness for mankind. Busloads of people travelled all around the country visiting the places where the statues were supposed to have moved. I know trustworthy people who still tell me they definitely saw such movement. They did see it happen, but whether through suggestion or otherwise, they, I, nor anyone else will ever know for sure.

And many people still believe priests have greater power in healing than does the medical profession.

Just a year ago I was going for a walk near my home. The road is blocked off because they are building a superhighway where we used to pluck daisies and look for birds' nests. Now you have to climb over ugly barriers and 'Trespassers Will Be Prosecuted' signs. I was doing that when I met Kevin. He was a little bit arthritic but still he had the bike by the head and he looked doubtful. He brightened when he saw me.

'The very man,' he said. 'You're the very man who'll help me with the bike.'

I had never seen him before in my life and he told me he had never seen me either but I could help him anyway. I could help him get his bike over the obstacles that stood between him and his home at the other side of what will be a superhighway.

We got it over an iron barred gate with the signs on it and then we walked along the earth path. We wondered at the machinery. Giant pterodactyls pulling things out of the earth, and massive hammers driving things into it.

Kevin said, 'Well, did ye ever see the likes of that? What would you say to that.' That was his habit, I was to learn: to ask 'What would you think of that?' after everything.

He was sixty-five now. Apart from the arthritis he was quite fit, still able to ride the bike. No matter whatever happened to him he would never go to doctors again; he'd only go to priests, 'What would you think of that?'

He had his reasons. In his forties he had 'a bit of the nerves, don't you know', and he went to the doctor. The doctor put him on Valium and he went 'all strange' but he kept on 'em anyway. After a couple of years he couldn't give 'em up. He heard tell of a priest who had a cure. He went to him. 'What would you think of that?'

The priest opened the door and said: 'Come in, my good man.' He put his hands on Kevin's head and prayed away. Kevin rested his bike against his hip and held out his own hands to show me the way the priest did it. Well, as soon as he did Kevin felt himself change. He felt something brush across his stomach and he knew he was better. To let me know what he felt he called me close to him and rubbed his finger across the back of my hand: 'Now that's what I felt across my stomach when that priest prayed over me. What would you think of that?'

That night his father, who was dead a good many years, appeared to him. He stood at the end of a tunnel. He didn't say a word but Kevin saw him there at the end of the tunnel. 'What would you think of that?'

Then, years later, an 'ulster' developed on his ankle and he went back to the priest. This time the priest took a relic of St Anthony, 'a "rale" [real] old relic, going back hundreds of years', and he rubbed it around the 'ulster'. Kevin called me in to him again to demonstrate. He did the back of my hand again. He went around 'rale slow' the way the priest did, first in one direction and then in the other.

The 'ulster' cleared up.

It cleared up in exactly the same way the priest rubbed the relic around it 'rale slow' and from the outside in.

We were now at the second obstacle at the other side of the forbidden territory and we got the bike over the ditch there. Kevin then laid it against a tree to take off his shoe and sock to show me the site of the cure. 'Twas clearly visible, a red but cured area of shiny skin where once the 'ulster' was. 'What would you think of that?'

He said he thought 'be the look of' me that I thought too much. 'Thinking too much is "rale" bad for you.' He encouraged me to give it up. He asked me what I did and I said: 'I write.'

'Write,' he said, laughing. 'I'd be hard put to write me name. What would you be writing about now?'

'About Ireland.'

'And what would you be writing about Ireland?'

'Oh, you know, old times and the things people believed in.'

'Well I tell you "wan" thing. We were a healthier people before they brought in all them ol' doctors with their pills and tablets, ruining half the country with that ol' poison.'

Throwing his stiff leg over the bar he asked me what I thought of his contention. I said I thought the opinion he held was quite valid.

What would you think of that?

As men aged they mellowed. They conceded a bit to outward displays of piety and devotion. Still, there's only so far a self-respecting man can be expected to go.

CHAPTER SIX

'Making Moonshine in Manhattan'

'One night we were all sitting around the fire in Den Paaty's fine house, and didn't my mother herself ask the question? Typical of her; she licensed herself to indulge what I was denied. She smiled that half-foolish smile that could easily throw a person off guard. I knew it well. I had often yielded valuable secrets to that smile before I had time to stop myself. Her uncle made the same slip now.

'Tell us, Den Paaty, how did you make all the money over there?'

My mother didn't really die until 1999 but, fond of fame and drama, she always claimed to have gone down in the *Titanic*. I suppose she did, in a way. This is how it happened. She had relations in America and they asked for pictures. My maternal grandmother got a photographer to take the pictures. She considered it worth the expense because these relations used to send her clothes for her family of thirteen. She dressed her children up in the raiment they had sent her, had the photographs taken (that event would itself surely be high drama in 1912) and the resulting picture was dispatched to the 'Yanks'. They never arrived, so my mother claimed that the picture of her and her siblings went down in the *Titanic*.

Maybe it did.

Mother definitely went out in the tender from Cobh (pronounced 'cove', then called Queenstown, and later pronounced Cob-H by many an American), near Cork – a major port of embarkation for emigration – to meet a liner bound for New York about thirteen years later, when she was sixteen. She was seeing her sister off. The plan was the sister would go out, save enough money and send it home to my mother so that she could follow her.

It didn't happen. I don't know exactly why. It could be that Nell (the sister who went) never got around to saving the money; it could be that she never sent it; or it could be another reason to do with my mother and some young man. I always suspected it was. She was secretive about the reason, 'Don't be bothering me, how do I know why I didn't go, I 'spose I hadn't the money.' That's what she'd say when I asked her. She got so bothered by the question I suspected there was a well-remembered reason but one that she didn't want to tell.

The Irish love the romance of 'going to America' and the stories that abound on the subject. Like any small boy growing up in rural Ireland, I was no exception. I asked my mother many times about 'going to America'. She would tell me a certain amount, about the 'American wakes' and about going down to Cobh. But then, on closer

The Titanic. It called into Cobh before the disaster that befell it. It wasn't a bit like the ships that took those fleeing famine in Ireland in the 1840s. The only similarity it had with the 'coffin ships' was that some of them sank to the bottom of the sea, too.

The evacuation of the remaining Great Blasket islanders in 1953. Families had been leaving, one or two at a time, for a number of years. They went mostly to Springfield, Massachussetts and Hartford, Connecticut

questioning about why she didn't go, she'd shut down with another 'Don't be bothering me ...'

Emigration started way back in the time of the Famine in the mid-19th century. The staple of the Irish diet was potatoes and the people lived mostly on 'spuds and milk'. Then for three successive years between 1846 and 1849 the potato crop failed, thanks to potato rot, called *Phytophthora infestans*, first reported in Ireland in 1845. For the first year people survived on what was left over from the previous one but when stocks ran out there was nothing to eat.

Either you starved or you emigrated.

The scale of this disaster, more than a century and a half later, is hard to grasp. Between the time of the Famine and 1900 it is estimated that Ireland's population halved, from about eight million to about four. In fact, Ireland was the only country in Europe whose population declined constantly from 1848 until the mid-1960s. Many of the emigrants tended to be young: 'The pick and flower of the land, so to speak, are going.' They went to many countries but America (that was how they invariably referred to the USA) was the favoured destination for it had the reputation of being a great place. Without doubt it was a better option than staying at home and facing at best hunger, at worst death.

They went on awful ships. They were desperate. The priority was raising the fare; once they had that they weren't too choosy about how they got there; they took what was going. Many of the boats never arrived, some of them sinking just a few days out of port. The ships that did make the crossing often delivered their passengers in a sore state, seriously sick and dying. So bad were the conditions on such boats that they called them 'coffin ships'.

One unnamed vessel was just out of port when she sank. Those

We don't know much about this picture except it was taken at the end of the nineteenth century. Houses were small; families were big – it looks like this strong woman has eight children and that she might be thinking of having another one.

This picture was taken on board a Norwegian motor vessel named Victory at Cobh on its way to Canada.

seeing their loved ones off were still standing on the quay waving goodbye when the ship went down. Another, the *Annie Jones*, sank on 29 September 1853, with the loss of 348 lives.

For the ships that did make it safely out of port, the crossing to America was both long and dangerous for vessel, crew and passenger. For these ships were, in general, never designed to carry passengers; they were built for cargo. They had a shallow draught because they were intended to make their way into shallow ports and, in some cases, up river. However, shipping merchants saw the opportunity to cash in on the situation; the boats took passengers west across the Atlantic and returned home to ports in England laden with timber and other cargo.

Peter O'Connor, a leading Sligo merchant, ordered the 276-ton barque *Industry* to be built in 1839 with just such a shallow draught to carry a cargo of Canadian timber through the channel in the bay, and up the river to his sawmills, at all levels of the tide. With the coming of the Famine and the high demand for passenger places, O'Connor saw the economic sense in filling the boat on both journeys. *Industry* started carrying passengers out and cargo home. We can only imagine the effects of the shallow draught of the ship on a westbound passage out of Sligo across the heaving Atlantic. One hundred and eighty-four emigrants from Sligo to New York embarked on 26 December 1846 under the command of Captain Michael Kelly. During the crossing, *Industry* ran into a succession of storms which allowed little progress. Over three long winter months the ship floundered at sea; food and water ran low, and even with the introduction of strict rationing two seamen and fifteen passengers died from malnutrition. *Industry* reached New York on 11 April 1847, after 106 days at sea.

Many Irish emigrants went to the US via Canada to avoid restrictions on entry, for not all US harbours welcomed Irish emigrants. Canada was less choosy. All passengers were supposed to be given a medical examination on arrival; if they had typhus or other diseases they could be, and often were, refused entry. Certain Canadian port authorities were deemed to be less selective than their US counterparts and many an Irish immigrant used Canada as a back door.

There were good ships as well as bad. One of them, the *Jennie Johnson*, never lost a member of crew or a passenger in all her numerous crossings during the time of the Famine. This distinction is now being honoured in Tralee, County Kerry, where a replica of the *Jennie Johnson* is being built, converted from cargo to passenger ship. It is hoped that in the near future it will make a crossing of the Atlantic with a selection of distinguished (and, no doubt, high paying) passengers to commemorate those who crossed in more perilous times for a somewhat lower fare.

Among this batch of Famine emigrants were Patrick Kennedy (the son of a tenant farmer from County Wexford), great-grandfather of the future American President, and John Ford, the father of Henry Ford, the pioneering car manufacturer, who had emigrated to America from Ballinacarty, County Cork, in 1847, having been evicted from his smallholding. Among those who emigrated some time later was John Bernard Kelly, father of Grace Kelly. He left Knock, County

Something tells me these passengers on board the Victory at Cobh on its way to Canada are not fleeing from famine. They look like they paid their own penny for the tickets – and the hats.

Mayo, at the turn of the century and eventually established a brick-laying firm in Philadelphia. But not all were destined for fame and fortune, or to sire celebrated sons or daughters. Mostly they had difficulty in finding jobs and places to live. Truth is, the Irish had a bad reputation. They were thought to be a bad lot, prone to excessive drinking and fighting.

Although my mother nearly went to America herself in the 1930s, things in Ireland weren't quite so bad as they had been during the Famine years. Still, it is hard for us to grasp how different life was then, even in her youth in the twenties and thirties. Families were large – anything under six was considered indecent, huge families in times when the average age for marriage was thirty-five for men and thirty for women. There was no work for the children when they grew up. There was no industry to speak of in rural Ireland; therefore, you either worked on the farm or emigrated. In big families, only one boy was destined to inherit the farm; the others had to emigrate. The girls had to go too, unless a match could be made for them with an inheritor of some neighbouring farm.

Farming was not a remunerative business either, so in many cases whole families went. Around poorer parts of Ireland, along the west coast especially, empty and abandoned houses were a common sight. When you came upon such places you'd see the older people nod their heads sadly and mutter something about 'gone to America, God help us'. That wasn't too long ago at all.

Although the 'American wakes' were held way back before my day, I am told they were times of mixed emotions. When someone was leaving it was the same as dying: no one believed they would ever come back. A party was given the night before where the old people mourned, sobbed and drank bottles of porter while the young ones sang songs and danced. The next day the emigrant was accompanied to Cobh by parents, brothers and sisters. Depending on how many passengers there were, they might be allowed out on the tenders.

The tenders were the small boats that took the passengers and

Small boats like the Glasgow seen here, took passengers and mail out to the big liners that anchored further out in deeper waters. These boats were called 'tenders'.

those seeing them off out to the big liner. The ships that did the Atlantic crossing were too big to get into the port. That's how my mother went out with Nell, on the tender, when she was going to America in 1925. Nell never came back. She was very sick on the crossing and nearly died. Less than a year later she married a fellow immigrant and eventually had seven children. In the fifties one of them was supposed to come and visit us but Nell changed her mind about sending her. She wrote to us asking if we had an inside lavatory. We hadn't, so the daughter never came. Nell said she couldn't have her daughter going out into the haggard (the stackyard). I thought they must be very posh if they could afford to be so finicky.

At the end of the sixties I went to Boston myself and looked up Nell. She lived in Charlestown. I found her in a one-bedroom apartment reached by stairs of stone with iron railings. The apartments were supplied by some public authority to those who couldn't afford to pay their own rent. It had an inside lavatory, all right. While I was there the daughter who hadn't visited us came to see her mother and told me she now had seven children herself and lived in an apartment much the same as her mother's, only it had more bedrooms.

But those who emigrated that far back sometimes did return. My mother told me about the ones who did and how they impressed everyone with all the good things they brought with them. She said that on the night of Nell's American wake a neighbour said to her, 'I suppose you'll be back in a few years with boxes of clothes.' That didn't happen. Poor Nell never came back – she's buried there now – but an uncle of my mother's did return.

She was very proud of him. He bought a farm near Cork city. Whenever we were going to have a day in the city we stayed in his house the night before. It was, to my young eyes, a very grand place. The night we'd be there we'd be allowed to stay up late and listen to him talking; he even had a touch of the American accent. He loved talking, and he was awful good at it. He'd lean back in the chair and hold his braces while he told us about America. To me it was not just the New World he was talking about; it was another world altogether, a world of cars and bright lights and exotic people. Listening to him was better than looking at the pictures in the few storybooks that were available to us – timid affairs with very ordinary people. He said there were black people in America. That put the tin hat on it: another world indeed!

He talked about New York and how high the buildings were: they were so tall you couldn't see the sky. He said the Irish over there were so lonely and they all lived only to get enough money to come home again. I thought they must be a hard lot to please if they wouldn't be satisfied with buildings that high. I had never seen anything more than three storeys high and thought I would forgo looking at the sky if I had such fine edifices to admire.

There was much speculation about how the people made money over there. Many of them sent parcels of clothes home, and there was a bit of a mystery about them, too. People wondered how they could possibly be 'casting off' what were considered nearly perfect garments. What activities they engaged in to be able to afford such fine things was a source of much wonder. My mother had always said

Irish emigrant clam diggers on Boston Harbour 1882. Despite the curiosity and suspicion about how some of those who emigrated made their money in America, the fact is most of them did it by hard labour over long hours.

there was some mystery about Den Paaty's (that was his name) money. When I showed interest in the hint of illegality and posed some pertinent questions I got another 'Don't be bothering me ...'

In the end I found out, anyway.

One night we were all sitting around the fire in Den Paaty's fine house, and didn't my mother herself ask the question? Typical of her; she licensed herself to indulge what I was denied. She smiled that half-foolish smile that could easily throw a person off guard. I knew it well. I had often yielded valuable secrets to that smile before I had time to stop myself. Her uncle made the same slip now.

'Tell us, Den Paaty, how did you make all the money over there?'

He wasn't prepared for the directness of it, it threw him, his defences were at rest and out came the answer. 'I made it making moonshine, Nora Latty (that was the mother's name) and I left with a gun to my arse.'

She was shocked to the core and I got the brunt of her shock. She grabbed me out of the stool I was perched on and fussed me up the stairs in front of her muttering, 'Language like that in front of the child ...' When she got me into bed I asked her what 'moonshine' was and she had no qualms about enlightening me.

'Moonshine is poteen, child, didn't you know that?'

Then she got serious and told me never to use the word Den Paaty used. 'That is only for grown-up men; good boys never use language like that.'

My mother had no trouble with her uncle brewing illicit alcohol in Manhattan but she wasn't going to have a son of hers saying 'arse'.

*

They immigrated to other places, too. Many went to Britain – to Liverpool, Manchester, Glasgow and London. There were no wakes for them. The trip was much shorter and mostly they came back every year or so. Indeed, some of them came and went more than once a year.

The tradition of going to England and coming home again had been

OPPOSITE:
Connoisseur and admirer. Not everyone knew what a good drop of poteen should taste like. It took a delicate palate and a caste iron stomach.

If steam rose up out of it it could be dangerous, you'd have to leave it another while to mature.

long-standing. Back at the beginning of the 19th century people had been going to England on a temporary basis. Many fathers from the west of Ireland came home in the spring to plough, sow and reap and then they would head off again, maybe in October. There was nothing to be done on the land in the winter so they spent it working on building sites or in factories in Britain when they had done what was to be done on whatever bit of land they had in Ireland. Then there were the people who went to pick potatoes. They went just for that season when the potatoes were ready for harvesting. They often went in family groups. This was a common tradition especially from Donegal. The task they did was called 'tatty-pickin''.

I was surprised on a recent visit to Donegal to meet a bus on the road announcing 'Glasgow' as its destination. I laughed to myself at the obvious mistake: how could a bus from Ardragh be going to Glasgow? When I got to the next town I went into a shop for a paper and got talking to the woman. I told her about what I had seen and expected her to laugh, too. She saw no fun at all in it. She said, 'Aiyee, that'll be for Glasgow all right, and if you want Edinburgh you'll find one later in the day.' When I asked her why, she explained the tradition of 'tatty-pickin''. She said since those days the tradition of going to Scotland still stood. And, she said, it was easy enough to get there; the sea crossing from Larne was only fourteen miles.

So, tradition, convenience and cost played a large part in determining where the emigrants went. England, being just a few hours across the water, was a popular destination. Yet, even though it was only a short crossing, and in theory easy, it could be rough. I don't know the reason but until recent times there was no day crossing. The mail boat went at night from Dun Laoghaire, the port just six miles south of central Dublin. The crossing took less than four hours but because of the late start one arrived in Holyhead at two or three in the morning. There was always a delay on the train. It was supposed to meet the boat but it was never there.

The first time I went was in 1956, when I was still a young boy. When we got off the boat we had to wait for more than an hour for the train. When it did chug in there was an awful scramble for seats. Half the passengers were left standing for the six-hour journey to

London. It was supposed to be six hours but it took eight. I don't know if there was any truth to it, but people used to say it was because we were Irish. They used to say that British Rail had much better service on other routes, that they put the worse trains on for the Paddys and that they didn't care whether the train was late or how long they took. That probably is not true, but it is an indication of the lack of trust that existed between the two nations. The boat from Cork was a lot worse. It took nine hours because it had to go around the eastern corner of the country before it crossed over.

Going to England was not a bit like going to America. Because it was a close destination it was cheap to get there.

People used to say those who could afford the money went to America and those who couldn't went to England. There was at least an inference that a different class of people went to the two destinations. It wasn't as easy to go to America in another way, too. Someone had to claim you and you had to do a 'Consul'. Doing a 'Consul' involved visiting the American embassy and having a medical examination.

There was no test for going to England; you just bought the ticket

A black Jamaican in the midst of Irish emigrants was not typical; we can see the novelty factor of it in the faces of these drinking men. The Irish in London worked hard, earned plenty of money, sent some of it home and drank the rest of it among themselves. They didn't integrate well.

Mrs Bridget Casey, of County Cork, Ireland, with her nine children, arrive in New York on S.S. Berlin. They are enroute to Bridgeport, Connecticut where the father has been residing with two other children, May, 22, and Margaret, 18, for the last four years. The second eldest child Bridget, 19, was left in Ireland having failed to pass the Immigration Department test.

and went. You didn't have to know anyone there to claim you in. Everyone was entitled to go; that was part of an agreement between the two countries. You didn't even have to know how to get there. In the sixties and seventies many widowed mothers made the crossing to be with their married daughters 'over there' for Christmas and a bit of the winter after it. It would be cold at home and they'd be saving the firing by going over. They'd take a turkey or goose with them. I remember one old woman telling me how easy it was to do it. She said, 'All I do is get on the train and follow the crowd – shure aren't we all going to the one place.'

There was prejudice on the Irish part about the English. Mostly it was about religion. Ireland was fundamentally Roman Catholic, England was 'pagan'. That is how many Irish people saw it. If you didn't go to mass on Sunday that's what you were – a pagan. There was a great danger of losing the faith in that country. Strangely, they did not think the same about America, or if they did it was not said. It may be that they thought if you lost the faith in America at least no one would know about it. What the neighbours knew and thought was always of paramount importance. If someone lost the faith in England it would be found out and that would be an awful slur on the family.

The Legion of Mary was a religious organization of voluntary lay people, founded by Frank Duff, who had been born in 1899 into a middle-class family. His followers called themselves Soldiers of Mary and they were very interested in saving everyone's souls. To the Soldiers of Mary, going to England involved risking eternal damnation. They used to hang around the point of embarkation watching for young people going to England. If they saw a young girl on her own they would approach her and question her about her destination, asking her why she was going. Often they would try to dissuade her. If they failed in that they would offer her an address in London where she could go. It was usually the address of some convent offering hostel accommodation.

Barrack Street Cork in full flow of diverse traffic: horse and cart, hand barrows, pram with bag of coal, bicycle and shank's mare. A motorized van brings up the rear.

If a girl did go to England on her own, her departure was inevitably surrounded by suspicion. Because, although no one admitted it openly, Irish boys and girls were capable of having sex, too. An Irish politician in the sixties famously said, 'There was no sex in Ireland 'til television.' I think most suspected he was not correct in this. So, if a girl was going to England on her own there was a question hung over the 'why' of it.

She might be pregnant.

Ironically, if a girl was discovered by her family to be in that condition, they would likely force her to go if they couldn't persuade the perpetrator of her condition to marry her. But if she was going of her own accord they tried to stop her in case she was pregnant and was going before anyone had the chance of sending her.

In contemporary Irish fiction, both Edna O'Brien and William Trevor have written extensively and affectingly about their homeland. Trevor's 1994 prize-winning novel, *Felicia's Journey*, tells of seventeen-year-old Felicia's journey of hope on the evening ferry across the Irish Sea to the post-industrial Midlands of England to find her lover and tell him she is pregnant. Regardless of the period in which the story is set, it is one with message that resonates up and down the decades.

People who went to England usually came home once a year. You'd see them at the mass. The clothes always gave them away; they would be brighter than the rest. The girls would have high heels and you'd hear them clicking their way up the church. The men, too, would be different; the suits would be good and they'd have hair oil in the hair and maybe a handkerchief poking out of the breast pocket.

They immigrated to other places, too. They went to Australia and New Zealand and many parts of the world, even to places like Argentina. I was in Argentina in the year 2000. I was there for St Patrick's Day and wrote an article on Ireland for an English language newspaper in Buenos Aires. While there, I was tracked down by descendants of Irish immigrants. They dined and wined me and treated me like a king. There is this enclave of Irish Argentinians who are

Irish emigrant waving goodbye to his family, leaving his island home on the first leg of a long trip to Australia.

passionate about their roots. If they meet a 'genuine' Irish person they take you to their homes and gather there others with similar roots. I was kept going for days. The ones who met me in Buenos Aires made me promise to call on their relations in Tuerta Vuelerta who sent me to their cousins in Rosario who phoned their friends in Cordoba to meet me off the bus.

Emigration to Argentina started more than a hundred years ago. I met one lady in her seventies who was fourth-generation Argentinian. She spoke English with an Irish accent and she spoke a little Irish, too. She danced an Irish jig, which she had learned in her youth from her parents in Argentina. They had learned it, she told me, from their parents in the city where they do the tango on the street. Before I left she made me promise that I would do all I could to let the people of Ireland know about this enclave of Irish Argentinians whose roots are their most important asset.

That is what she said. I didn't doubt her. I went to mass with her. Afterwards, the congregation met and greeted each other outside the church as I had seen my own relations do in Ireland long ago. We don't do that any more but these Irish Argentinians do – and all of them speak the way the seventy-year-old lady did, with an Irish accent.

But everything has changed now.

Now the traffic has turned and people from all over the world are coming to Ireland to work. That trend started just before the turn of the 21st century. The first I knew of it was September 1999. I live in a little village about thirty miles from Dublin. Despite the 'Celtic tiger' economy advance, there was little evidence in my sleepy little village that anything had changed dramatically. The main road from Dublin to Cork runs through the heart of the village and I had noticed an increase in the traffic there; I had heard on the news that the long period of depression was over, that we were out of the slump, but I wasn't prepared for what my sister told me. I am interested in things Russian and speak a little of the language. She came to me one evening and, pointing to a house a few yards from my flat, she said, 'I heard there are five Russian men living in that house'. She is normally a sensible sober woman but I looked at her for signs of drink taken.

Negative!

I asked her to repeat and she did, and added that she heard they were working in the local factory, the only one in the village. She said they couldn't get anyone to work now, that they had to import labour. When she was gone I took myself in the direction of the house. It was dusk. There were three men crouched smoking outside the front door. I had seen Russian men in this kind of crouch in parts of Russia.

I said, 'Hello!'

No response.

I tried again, 'Nice evening, isn't it?'

Nothing.

Though I thought it a little insane I decided to try it anyway – 'Zdrasvoute!'

They came to life. They smiled all around and approached me to tell me how glad they were to hear someone speak their language. Between them they had not a word of English. They were the first of the new immigrants I met. Ironic, but in my own little village just thirty miles from Dublin I got more opportunity to speak Russian that I had in three months in Siberia a couple of years before.

Now the place is truly cosmopolitan. On Dublin's streets it seems like a quarter of the population is foreign. There are black and yellow faces, oriental eyes and strange robes. Many are asylum seekers; others come seeking work in the new and prosperous Ireland. Recently, as I was writing one day, I heard music. I got up to look out of the window and investigate its source. There is a girls' school across from my flat. Before that day I didn't know it had a band; it has and it is good. The girls were parading around the schoolyard in fine formation. A few played flutes, some blew bagpipes, others squeezed accordions. Proudest of all was a beautiful black girl fairly beating the big base drum with Scoil Bridhe Naofa (St Brigid's School) emblazoned on its side.

I remembered Den Paaty saying that there were black people in New York and I thought that I couldn't wait to be big enough to go and see such a wonder. They say if you wait long enough for something it will come to you.

Despite the comfort of the chair this boy looks a little lost and lonesome in Dublin's Liberties. I don't know when it was taken but a flat now, where he sat then, forlorn, would fetch a fancy penny.

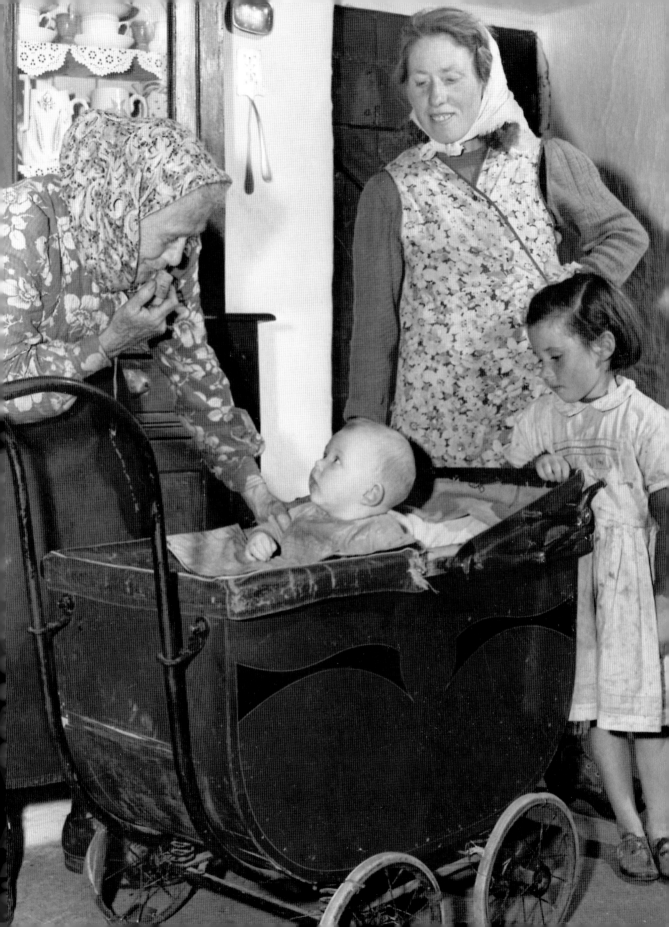

CHAPTER SEVEN

Dublin Pawn Shops and Perambulators

'Of course, the residents of inner Dublin didn't have a car, but they all had a pram. The pram was a very important vehicle. It was used for the babies when they were young but when they grew out of it it did not go into disuse. No indeed! It was used for carrying coal and messages (the shopping). It was especially convenient for 'spuds' and vegetables; and where would a woman be without a pram to take her pawnable goods around to the shop with the three balls outside it of a Monday morning?'

OPPOSITE:
Going to the pictures was a favourite hobby of those living in Dublin. Courting couples always went of a Sunday night. 'Twas a safe enough pastime, the censors scissors saw to it that they were not exposed to evil, foreign influences – like sex for example.

These wee boys in York St. Dublin look like they are not going to yield an inch; too often their city was whipped from under them, first by foreign invaders, then by culchies (country people).

It is not without reason that Dublin was always a little sensitive to strangers. When the Vikings settled there in 837 it took rather a long time to persuade them to go home. It wasn't until Brian Boru defeated them at the Battle of Clontarf in 1014 that the Irish regained their capital city. Even then, the remnants of Scandinavian rule remained. On St Matthew's Day, 21 September 1170, the last Norseman, Hasculf McTorkil, finally handed over his control of the city. But to whom did he hand it over? Another foreigner: Strongbow. He was the Norman nobleman who had landed in Waterford in 1169. As a prize for his conquest he took the hand of Aoife, one of the fairest Irish maidens, in marriage. Now another foreigner was giving this foreigner the city of Dublin. The descendants of the new foreign occupier held the city for nearly eight hundred years. That is probably why they are still a little scared of visitors. It would seem those who come are not inclined to leave.

An old friend died recently in his eighties. He was born a Cork man, he became a policeman and he lived all his working life in Dublin. He loved to tell me over and over again what a great place Dublin was and how good-natured were its citizens. He'd always start off by telling about the time, in the early forties, when he first came up to Dublin to train in the depot there. He got off the train at Kingsbridge Station and walked with his suitcase the half-mile to the barracks he was to live in during his training. On the street was a bunch of young Dubliners playing with a ball. The new recruit was full of camaraderie, and, it being his first time in the city, he thought he would greet the playing ones the way he would have greeted any stranger in the Cork town he had come from.

Dubliners were full of heart; if they had they gave, if they hadn't they expected others to do the giving.

'Are ye having a good time?' he asked, with a patronizing smile.

Everything came to a halt. Even the ball stopped. When he used to

tell the story he'd stop himself for a full half-minute before he delivered their response, in a bad Dublin accent (it's not a thing you learn in sixty or seventy years; it comes in the genes); he'd tell me this, as if I hadn't heard it a hundred times before:

'Jaysus Christ! Another culchie. Will yis go back to where ye came from.'

There was no malice in it. The Dubliners didn't hate the culchies (that is what they called people from the country), they just didn't understand them, and they thought they would never make it in Dublin. They thought culchies would feel as out of place in the city as Dubliners did the odd time they went to the country.

People were secretive about who they voted for themselves but curious to find out where others put their mark.

I don't think the Dubliners hated anyone; they were full of good heart, but they didn't understand life outside the city. They were very open; they didn't know why country folk kept secrets. Dubliners told everything out straight. Even problems in the home were reported without embarrassment. Country people had many skeletons in the cupboard: a family member who died of consumption; a sister who went to England 'under very peculiar circumstances'; an aunt who left the nuns.

The city itself was a very small place in those days. There were no suburbs. What became suburbs in the fifties and sixties were, before that, villages far from the city. Real Dublin consisted of the Liberties (an area of artisan dwelling just south of the Liffey) and a few Georgian streets and squares just north of it. Well, there were other Georgian streets and squares on the south side, too – Merrion Square and Fitzwilliam Square – but they were for the rich and only 'half-Irish' people like Oscar Wilde, W.B. Yeats, George Russell (AE) and other literati who lived, talked and wrote there. Genuine Dubliners (Dubs, as they like to be called) lived in tiny houses in the Liberties, or in a large room in one of massive Georgian buildings north of it. In the 19th century these fine buildings had been the dwelling places of rich families. Each house was occupied by a single family and its servants. In the Dublin of later years, they were occupied by many families, one to each room, or, at most, a couple of rooms. The once elegant rooms were their homes, the stairways were their meeting, courting and arguing grounds.

These Dubs hardly ever went to the country. Maybe on a warm August weekend they might prise 'hisself' off the high stool in the local pub and persuade him to go to the seaside for a couple of days. It they did they always took a few 'mammies' with them. Dubliners were great respecters of 'mammies'. On a trip they would take not only the real mammy of the family, but her mammy also. There might even be a few stray mammies from the rooms above or below, or maybe a mammy who lived on her own. And if there were a mammy who had bronchitis ('bad bronichals') anywhere in the vicinity she would have to be brought along, too.

Very many Dubliners, especially the elderly, had 'bad bronichals', from the city pollution. Coal was burned in profusion. People coughed and wheezed a lot. They slapped themselves on the chest, and might ask you to give them a clap on the back to help them bring up the 'ol' flem'. Bronchitis was widespread and chronic and was known as the 'bad 'ol' bronichals'. Constipation was another problem but it afflicted the young more than the old. Whether affected or not, every child in those times took a weekly 'dose'. It could be of cod liver oil or Beecham's Powders or laxative coated with chocolate; it might even be a kind of tea made from senna pods. Whatever the chosen remedy, every child had to have his or her weekly dose of it.

The trip to the seaside was a mini safari. Tin buckets and wooden spades were packed in with swimming togs, or, in their absence, undergarments that would pass for swimming attire. The cases, the mammies and his complaining self ('Jaysus, how did I let meself get talked into this'), urged on by the excited young, boarded the bus for Bray, twelve miles south of Dublin, by the sea in County Wicklow. The more adventurous, if they had an extra few bob, might go as far south as Courtown in County Wexford for the few days.

Human nature being what it is, as soon as they got there they'd want to come back. But they couldn't do that. If they returned the same day as they went the neighbours would be laughing at them and the bus

A noonday nap.

fare would be gone to waste. So, they forced themselves to tough it out.

During the day, if it didn't rain, the mammies were parked on the sand. They took off their shoes and pulled their dresses above the knees to let the sun at the varicose veins. Trying to keep the wind from blowing the hair into their eyes they'd compare the ABC on their shins and keep an eye on the children who'd be splashing and fighting in the water. The children would be so charged with excite-

ment the mammies would be terrified they would go too far out. They'd have to interrupt their talk about the veins and ABC to shout warnings at the young ones: 'Don't be going an' drowning yerselves now, I'm warning you! – If you drown I'll kill you.'

The men would wander around half-lost. They'd struggle to walk on the sand and they'd keep an eye out for another exile they could complain to about how they were forced into the excursion.

At night they all went to the pub. This was the men's opportunity to

ABOVE: Dubs went to Bray mostly. Riding the donkey was a novelty for the children and it gave the parents a rest, too. They could stop watching out for them to drown for a while.

LEFT: Cork people went to the seaside, too. They were always more fussy than Dubs about what they wore and the impression they were making. Here, a group descends the train at Youghal, hair coiffed, dresses starched and ironed – we're even wearing pearls.

If the sun shone Dubliners felt they had to go to the seaside, but they didn't like exposing themselves to the hazards of travelling 'down the country'. Portmarnock was a great place for them to go; they could take a double decker bus out there, or even cycle to it.

complain. The pint wasn't good. Dubliners considered Guinness's brewery to be their private source of consolation. The stuff was made in Dublin for Dubliners. It didn't travel, they'd tell you. The stuff was available in the country, but, like countrymen in Dublin, Guinness down the country was out of place. It wasn't the real stuff at all. They were drinking it just so as not to upset the publican. They said it was all right for the women because they drank bottled Guinness, out of refinement, and the stuff you got out of bottles was safe enough. It was the men who had to take the risk. The belly you might get from a bad pint could be a dangerous thing. Indeed, many's the Dublin man who picked up a nasty dose in the country.

The lot returned to the capital red from the sun, bloated with

OPPOSITE:
Artist takes a break for inspiration! Raddler, James Maher, marking the rim of casks to indicate their contents at Guinness brewery at Saint James' Gate, Dublin.

Though now 'tis made in many different places and taken all over the world, Guinness's best porter was first made in Dublin for Dubliners; it didn't travel well.

indigestion from the bad drink and the country food, but very happy to be back in civilization. Once home, they'd start coughing and wheezing with renewed vigour and swear that they would never again 'go down the country'.

Dublin is divided in two by the River Liffey. It flows through the centre. The bridge that links the two halves of the city is called O'Connell Bridge, named after Daniel O'Connell, 'The Liberator', the Kerry lawyer (another out-of-towner) who claimed he could drive a horse and four through any Act of British Parliament. And this he did, more or less; he won some degree of freedom for Irish Catholics in the Catholic Emancipation Act of 1829. Ironically, the bridge named after the man, and down upon which his statue gazes, is now a formidable barrier between the two halves of the city. You can cross it easily enough – no one will stop you doing that – but will you ever conquer the divide?

They say O'Connell Bridge over the Liffey is the only bridge in Europe that is wider than it is long. Now that to me is very strange, because, metaphorically speaking, the Liffey must be the widest river in Europe; one would expect it would take an awful long bridge to span it. It was crossed with the same trepidation as one expects from a crosser of the Styx. In older times people from north of the river were, to the southsiders, only a kick in the ass from being a culchie. Dublin people never married culchies, and they seldom married anyone from the other side of the river. I think that had a lot to do with the closeness of family in those times.

The mammy was the centre of the group and her children were not prepared to wander too far from her, even in adult life. Only about twenty years ago I met a man in Sandycove, which is on the south side of Dublin. He was sitting on a bollard by a quay overlooking Dublin Bay. From there you can see all of the north side clearly. That is another strange thing: despite the great mental division that separates people from either side of the city, the physical gap is almost nothing. Sandycove, on the south side, is home to the Martello tower

The River Liffey awash with Guinness business. Thirst had little patience; it was full steam ahead to get the stuff to the consumer. A Dublin man could be marred for life by drought.

Taking it easy at the base of O'Connell's statue which overlooks O'Connell's Bridge which spans Dublin's River Liffey.

The most important Gaelic matches take place in Dublin's Croke Park. This is a hurling final between Cork and Wexford.

that James Joyce occupied. It is from here that Bloom starts out on his day's excursion that is the subject of Joyce's famous novel *Ulysses*. From Sandycove you can see clearly all the way to Howth and that, even today, is the most distant northern suburban. In olden times it was a far-off village. It was, and is, visible to the extent that you can make out the doors and windows in the houses over there. Well, the man I met wasn't looking that far off at all; he was only looking at Clontarf, the site of Brian Boru's success in expelling the first foreigners to occupy the city. The place is just three miles north of the centre. He was very dejected. He had a potbelly and a torn vest covering it. He had nothing else on top of him. His very white belly was protruding through the hole in the vest and this added to his down-and-out appearance.

'That's where I came from,' he said to me, pointing across the bay.

'Clontarf?'

'Yeah! Clontarf.'

The way he said it would bring a tear to any eye. Even if you did not know the place you'd know he loved it. I didn't know how to console him. He went on to tell me how, in arduous youth, he had married a Sandycove girl. Adventure had taken him across the river to see the other side. It was a sunny day and he came to play on the beach at Sandycove. There he met his wife, fell in love, and they married.

Now, years later, he sat in his vest, potbelly in evidence, gazing long-ingly as far north as he could to the place he'd strayed from, all those years ago.

And here at the same venue a football match between Dublin and Kerry.

Touched by his nostalgia I asked if he ever thought of taking his wife and family and going back to live over there. His jaw dropped and he looked at me to see if I was serious or sane. Then, realising I was a countryman and not altogether understanding of city ways, he said: 'She'd never leave the mammy.' As soon as he had said it I felt insensitive for not having known.

These close family ties peaked within the inner city. It was in these very poorest parts that the real old Dubs lived out their frugal lives. The frugalness didn't, however, impact on their capacity for enjoy-ment and wit.

In olden times (hundreds of years before the times I am talking about) penal codes forbade the use of Irish language and patriotic songs. The bards of the time found a way around this. They wrote songs and poetry about Ireland but they didn't call it Ireland; they

Hardy Old Dubs wrapped themselves well against the cold but they left it to Fate and Nature to protect them from other health hazards. Here butcher with 'fag' in mouth cuts meat for discerning customer who looks like he will only take a quality cut. Comfortable cat ignores all.

called the country by women's names – Cathleen ni Houlihan, Dark Rosaleen and others like that. One of these names was Kathleen Mavourneen. In a song dedicated to this Kathleen, there is a line that goes: 'It may be for years and it may be forever.' Dubliners' wit caught on to the sentiment and applied it to the more everyday aspects of their own life that often went on for years and, indeed, sometimes forever. They therefore called buying items on a weekly instalment plan the 'Kathleen Mavourneen'.

In thirties and forties Dublin, salesmen went around the Liberties and up and down the stairs of the tenements of North Great George's Street and Clanbrassil Street, selling items out of brown suitcases. Their terms of sale was the 'Kathleen Mavourneen'. Mostly, the salesmen were Jews. Obviously they were of an ecumenical disposition because the goods they had on offer consisted of holy pictures, statues, prayer books and rosary beads. St Patrick, pointing with clay fingers at snakes and telling them to 'be gone' from Ireland, was a big seller. St Anthony was good, too, and everyone had to have an Infant of Prague. If you put a thrupenny bit under the Infant you would never be without money. At least, that is what they used to say. The thing was, when you did have such a coin under the statue it was inclined to list; this made him unstable so that he was prone to tumbling down and losing his head. A statue with a head broken off at the neck was bad luck. The Infant of Prague needed lots of replacing – Jewish sellers loved the Infant.

Though religious paraphernalia was their main merchandise, they were not limited to this. Their range extended to shoe polish and brushes, pot scrubs, picture frames, blue for the whitewash, knickers, corsets, hair combs, cod liver oil, Sloane's liniment, candles, wicks for paraffin lamps and yards of material that could be made into shirts, dresses or curtains. They carried ready-made clothes, too. They'd have a few girls' white dresses that would do for confirmation or communion. They would provide suits for boys for the same events, but they did not carry these with them. They would use one of the tape measures that they had for sale to measure up the young chap and

In Dublin's Liberties 1950 when prams were an integral part of life and commerce. Where would you be without one? These girls must have used it to transport their goods to the point of sale. When custom is not over brisk one could always take a bit of a sit down in the 'ould' pram.

No shortage of shoes at 9s 11d and 10/=. This picture comes from 1946 when many goods were still rationed in neutral Ireland after the WWII. The excess may be due to the fact people used their coupons for things of greater necessity – food.

deliver the next time they came around to collect whatever was due on previous purchases.

Most old Dubs were tied up with 'Kathleen Mavourneen'. Every week the man with his brown suitcase came to collect their two shillings or half-a-crown (2/6d). He was quick to point out their reducing liabilities. He would tell them when they had only a few more months left to pay for their previous purchases, and he would encourage them to invest in another statue or something that would bring them luck and happiness. Plastic flowers must have marked a turning point in the market for the selling men. When they came into vogue in the fifties every flat in inner Dublin had them in the window between the lace curtain and the glass to give joy to themselves and passers-by.

Other important performers in the drama of tenement dwelling were the gas man, the coal man and the rent man.

Gas was metered and the meters took a penny. The man came every few weeks to empty the meters. He'd count out the money, stacking it into piles of twelve – twelve pennies equals one shilling. These stacks were put into paper bags and the paper bags were deposited in a case like a doctor's. Every gas man had such a case. The coal man rang a bell. He had his coal on a horse and cart; he rattled around the cobbled streets shouting out and ringing his bell. People flocked down the stairs with basins and buckets. The coal man weighed out the coal and loaded it into whatever receptacles the people provided. Coal men's teeth always looked very white because their faces were so black. People say the coal man was always smiling, but one observant type also remarked that that was only because you always saw his white teeth against the blackness of his face. This created the impression of a constant smile.

Of course, the residents of inner Dublin didn't have a car, but they all had a pram. The pram was a very important vehicle. It was

Overleaf:
'In Dublin's fair city, Where the girls are so pretty, I first laid my eyes on sweet Molly Malone'. Moore St. 1946 where the famed lady is said to have plied her trade of selling 'cockles and mussels alive alive – o'.

Early 1940s Dublin. The wooden trays were stacked on carriages drawn by horses over cobbled streets. The bread man wore a leather bag over his shoulder for the money. If people couldn't pay he wrote what they owed in a notebook. He kept the notebook in the bag with the money.

An elegantly dressed boss oversees an unintimidated 'gorsoon' worker at the Raleigh factory where they made bicycles.

used for the babies when they were young but when they grew out of it it did not go into disuse. No indeed! It was used for carrying coal and messages (the shopping). It was especially convenient for 'spuds' and vegetables; and where would a woman be without a pram to take her pawnable goods around to the shop with the three balls outside it of a Monday morning? What money there was would be spent by then so the pram would be loaded up with anything that wasn't needed for the immediate future. There might be candlesticks or accordions, fire irons or radios; and who needed 'hisself's' suit hanging on the back of the door from Monday to Friday when it could be earning its living in the pawn shop?

There were a few bicycles. A shop called McHugh Himself was well known to all Dubliners. There you could buy a bike for 2/6d a week. There were other shops, too, that geared their style of retailing with the customer in mind. Every shop had a copybook where goods bought 'on tick' (credit) were written in. Women could sometimes have difficulty in persuading shopkeepers of their creditworthiness. They used to encourage the owner to part with his goods, telling him they were better in use than sitting on his shelf. ''Twill go bad on the shelf, 'twon't go bad in the book', that's what they used to say.

It was in this tenement Dublin that Sean O'Casey (1880–1964) set his plays *The Plough and the Stars* and *Juno and the Paycock*. The settings themselves made for high drama – obvious former grandeur, and even more obvious present squalor, provided a wonderful backdrop for the action of the plays. The characters were outstanding and the lines were terrific. Real life within these same buildings was no less dramatic than the plays. The characters were as big, the lines were as good and the accent was as mellifluous. There also was great tragedy.

There was poverty, there was ill health, and, behind the loud laughter, there was the depression that shadows the poor everywhere in the world.

The government thought it would be a good thing to move the tenement dwellers out. Plans were drawn up to build houses far from the centre of the city. The government said that was the trend in other countries – to house people in the suburbs. The centre was henceforth to be for trade and enterprise. They thought it was a good plan. Maybe it was, maybe it was all that could have been done, yet it was very difficult for the Dubs to adapt to life away from their familiar landmarks.

One old Dublin woman remembered the day she was moved from her tenement to a small house in Goldenbridge. Seventy years after it happened she was still sad to the extent that she filled up with tears and had to stop here and there in the telling of the story. She was only ten herself when the move came about. She told about getting two

Time was a child could stay in a pram 'til she was three – four if she were small; then came the go-car. One had to transfer to it after a mere year of lying-down life. At about the same time they tried to get adults to move from Georgian buildings to boxes in the suburbs. Here we see both (child and adult) protest at perceived declining standards. This sit down in York St. Dublin was an attempt to halt the demolition of the Georgian buildings that had been their homes.

In McCurtain Street Cork in 1932 they were taking down tram wires. In 2003 they are talking about putting them back up again.

trams, one from O'Connell Street to Kelly's Corner and another from there to where they were sending her family to live. She said even Kelly's Corner (about one mile from the centre) was further than she had ever gone before. She said she had to wait so long there for another tram to take her even further out that she feared she would never again find her way back to the inner city where she was born and bred. She remembered carrying a green vase; her mother was carrying a pink and gold oil lamp. At the end of the line the tram man told them to get off; he said he wasn't going any further. This was Rialto, about three miles from Kelly's Corner. They walked to the house and when they got there her mother broke down, devastated. 'We are out in the country,' she said; 'we are so far from Dublin, I'll never be able to walk it, that's for sure.' The lady said that moving to 'the country' started them reading the papers. That was the only positive result this woman could remember about the move out – her parents started reading papers. They read the deaths column every day to see if any of their friends who had been scattered to other places had died.

New suburbs sprung up all over the place, equally awful in their sameness. There were strings and strings of 'little boxes', all the same, stretching for miles in all directions. The houses were adequate, no doubt, but the monotony of such a large number of them to this day mars the appearance of what were once individual villages.

Crumlin was one of the earliest areas to which the inner city people were sent. Hard to estimate how many houses were built: I only know that the few times I had to go through them to find some individual I felt I was in a maze. After some time going up and down streets, all the same, and asking people where such and such a road was, you're be really bamboozled. I remember thinking to myself, how do people find their way home? How do they not go into the wrong house? They are all so much the same and there are so many of them.

In his youth Brendan Behan (1943–64), author, poet, playwright and all-round hell-raiser, was sent off to Crumlin with his parents. Behan himself claimed to be basically homosexual. He made this claim in public and no one ever knew for sure if it were the case, and, as far as I know, it has never been confirmed. This claim might well have been made to shock. Brendan always made it in very public places and always in company. I believe he liked his claim to be heard by clerics. Though where he came within earshot of any 'of the cloth' is a mystery. Behan was very anti-cleric and anti-Catholic. True or not, Behan claimed that Eamon de Valera was responsible for his sexual orientation.

De Valera, leading member of the Easter Rising and later President of the country, was one of the main instigators of the scheme to move people from the centre to the suburbs. Behan used to say that De Valera's housing reform had ruined his ordinary sexual development. He said the move from the cosy slums out to the windy spaces of rows of houses in Crumlin had come at a crucial stage in his development and had been disastrous as far as his orientation was concerned. He used to say that on the landings and in the hallways of the tenements

Guard on duty in Dublin. Most guards came from the country and spent six months training 'in the depot' before they were released on the public to direct traffic with white gloves and generally help people. They were great for giving directions to other country folk who found themselves lost in the big city.

you could always get a grope and a squeeze, and that at fourteen he was just getting the hang of it when the move came along.

Another story that illustrates admirably the difference the scheme made to Dublin and its residents was told by a man who lived in Drumcondra. Drumcondra is about one mile north of the centre and would, in the early days of the 20th century, have been considered the very outer limits of the city. Beyond Drumcondra were fields, beyond these fields, Ballymun, a small village. Only forty years ago it was a farming area. The land there was very fertile and excellent for mushrooms. A friend who lived in Drumcondra had two sons and they loved mushrooms. There was no better place for them than the fields in Ballymun. One Sunday the son and a friend set off on bicycles to pick mushrooms there. They left too early to have mass, so the mother warned them that they were to go to mass somewhere along the way. They did. They went to mass in Ballymun. Later they picked their mushrooms. They gathered bushels of them and came home happy.

The next day my friend was at work in a factory somewhere in between Drumcondra and Ballymun and he was telling a colleague that his son had gone to pick mushrooms the day before in his area.

'Oh, that'll be who they are talking about,' the man from Ballymun said.

'What do you mean?' the friend asked.

'My daughters were at mass in Ballymun yesterday and they were saying that there were two strangers in the church. We couldn't figure out what two strangers would be doing in Ballymun of a Sunday morning. Now I know, it will have been your son and his friend out for the mushrooms.'

I didn't move to Dublin myself until the early sixties. People used to tell me that I had missed the best of it, that all the 'characters' had either died or moved on. Well, I don't think they had. At least I was in time to see Brendan Behan in operation. I used to go down Grafton Street and look into all the pubs with a reputation for having interesting customers. McDaid's was the big one. There wasn't a whole lot special about it as a building, and it wasn't on Grafton Street but Harry Street, off Grafton Street. My earliest memory of it is not of any personality in particular but of the number of pints of Guinness. They

Grafton St. was always elegant and full of fashion. The good drinking pubs like McDaid's and the Bailey were, appropriately, off the street. Thus, drunks didn't dirty and desecrate it, they only had to use it to waddle home on.

You could tell by the number of rings on a glass how many sups a man had taken to finish his pint. Henry Barter in John Mullet's in Amiens Street did it in three – then, it seems, he stopped for a pull on the pipe – 'shure you'd have to – you'd be jaded from it'.

were all over the place, on the counter, on the tables, on the shelves, and in everyone's hands. I remember thinking there were a lot more pints than people. I said this to the friend who was introducing me to the premises and he said 'Of course!'. I asked him what he meant and he said, 'These boys can't be waiting between pints, they'll have the next one ordered before they are halfway through the first one.'

I had already started drinking myself but I hadn't got as far as Guinness. The memories of my youth and men at fairs had kept me back from it. I thought it was black and evil and, no doubt, this impression was added to by my mother's contention that 'the devil himself was inside that black stuff'. That first day in McDaid's I buried all my former prejudices of the stuff and ordered half a pint. My friend blushed and told the barman I was 'new'. He nodded his understanding and plopped a full pint, still dripping creamy foam, down in front of me, claiming that what he was giving me was a pint 'I made meself'.

I liked it.

We had another. We talked. I fell into the atmosphere of the place. You could talk to anyone. Those who didn't feel like talking were stuck in newspapers and they dropped sheets of it all around them as they were finished. Those who weren't reading had bundled up papers stuck out of their pockets. Everyone was smoking. There were some females in the place. Sure-of-themselves females, not women looking to attract men, but women who had reached a distinct and obvious liberation before anyone started burning bras.

I had another few pints.

I swore to my companion about my conversion. I was a changed man. I would never drink any place again except McDaid's, and I would never touch a sup of anything else bar Guinness.

I was only just in bed when the room started to swim. I tried to steady it down by closing my eyes. It got worse. I decided to get up and try to stop it. The Guinness decided it was time to come up, too. It did. It took about the same length of time as it did to go down but it came in shorter and briefer instalments. To this day I have never drunk Guinness again, but I have been back to McDaid's.

Patrick Kavanagh drank there, too, as did almost everyone who had any claim to literary or artistic ability, revolutionary ideas or a past involvement in organizations such as the IRA. Brendan Behan was all of these. He had been interred for his involvement and he had also been to borstal. He was in fact barred from Britain for a long time. Even in my day they used to say that Special Branch men kept an eye on what was going on in McDaid's. Any stranger with a hat on drinking there would be pointed to with a whisper and a knowing nod – 'one of them'. I never believed it. I don't think they would ever have made any sense of what was being said or what was going on in that pub. From my experience it was impossible to distinguish who was what. There were those who claimed to be patriots willing to die for the cause. After an overdose of pints they'd shout 'Up the Republic' and 'Brits Out' but

Non-Dubliners drank, too. Some women did it. Top: O'Meara's College, Killarney. Bottom: Woman with blond hair, handbag, red nails and a smile drinks half a pint.

Processions provided a fine opportunity to parade fashion. Women had to cover their heads going into the church or attending outdoor religious ceremonies. If it were a rainy day they complied by wearing headscarves but if the sun shone at all out came the hats. Here we see them on a very fine day walking in Church Street in Dublin. The occasion is a celebration of the feast day known as Corpus Christi when processions were held all over the country.

they were quickly soothed by another creamy pint. They'd often lull into peaceful slumber. I don't think Kathleen Mavourneen could ever have relied on them to come to her protection even if she were in some great distress. Others claimed to be anarchists, Maoists, Communists, supporters of Che Guevara or anyone with an attractive name. The only common denominators I ever saw among the clients of McDaid's was a love of Guinness and talk.

McDaid's had a kind of annex where its regular clients had some claim to after-hours facilities. It was not an extension to the building, it wasn't even near it; it was a mile away in Fitzwilliam Street. It was an old Georgian building with basement kitchen, pantry wine cellar and various other dark and dank rooms. Here the regulars slept off the excess. They paid no rent. One man who claimed to have lived there for a few years told me the person who owned it did not need to charge rent. He said all they did was collect the empty bottles and

the refund on these paid for the place. There was no maintenance.

Brendan Behan officially lived in Crumlin with his exiled parents but he seldom made it home. He spent much of the fifties in the Catacombs (that is what this Georgian building was called).

McDaid's and other pubs in and around Grafton Street were the meeting places for those involved in literature, actors, layabouts and those wanting to observe these in their favourite activity of drinking and dreaming. Others met at the 'Pillar'.

The talented partnership of Hilton Edwards (standing) and Micheal MacLiammoir injected lifeblood into Dublin theatre of the 40s and 50s.

This was in the middle of O'Connell Street, which was deemed to be the centre of Dublin. It was 121 feet tall. Atop it, observing all with his one good eye, was Admiral Lord Nelson, hero of Trafalgar. Everyone in Ireland knew it. It was one common denominator between the separated societies of Dubliners and culchies; no matter where you were from, if you wanted to meet someone there was no better place than 'at the Pillar'.

Well! Up it went, and down it came in an explosion of 'patriotism'. More about that later.

If you walked directly north from the Pillar, past a monument to Charles Stuart Parnell, past the Ambassador Cinema, past the Rotunda, the first maternity hospital in Dublin which, at its opening, boasted 'only two to a bed', and past the Gate Theatre, founded by Michael McLiammoir and his lover Hilton Edwards, you'd come to a street called Montgomery Street. It was famous for other kinds of meetings. Generally known as 'Monto', it was home to sixteen hundred prostitutes, the largest red light district in Europe in the first half of the 20th century.

The work of Frank Duff 's Legion of Mary has been mentioned in the previous chapter in relation to the concern he and his followers showed for young girls leaving the country for England. Closer to home, Frank found that unwed mothers had a terrible time of it. These women were total outcasts. Many of them arrived at the state

By 1960s the miniskirt had made it to Ireland but white dresses, veils and nuns habits (long) were still in vogue.

they were in as a result of plying the oldest of all trades 'up in Monto'. Frank decided he would make it his battleground.

The Legion of Mary was dedicated to helping not only the poor and needy but especially the women involved in prostitution. Homes were opened for unmarried mothers and their babies. Some of Frank's Soldiers of Mary worked in the homes. Other privates of this army marched on Monto. Their job was to try to convince the ladies on parade there that greater and more enduring reward sprung from serving Mary than Mammon. This was in times before contraception, so the armour the Soldiers of Mary dispensed consisted of rosary beads and medals with Our Lady on one side and a cross and heart on the other. They were called miraculous medals and miraculous they must have been because Monte was cleaned up. By the 1950s, it was a lifeless place, bereft of trade. It had become another of those places people love to talk about – 'part of Dublin city in the rare ol' times'. All those who drank at McDaid's and other watering holes around Grafton Street claimed to have been habitués of the place. Even those so young they would have to have been born adolescents rather than infants to make the claim plausible.

And now the Pillar.

The distrust that existed between those on either side of the river – almost a superstition – was taken on by the culchies (me included) who came into the city. When I was a student, my best friend warned me never to take home a girl from a dance unless I knew exactly where she was from. He never did. Girls from the north side, he used to say, were nothing but trouble. He also used to say he felt it was unlucky to have anything to do with someone from 'over there'. I think there was a practicality involved, too. There was no public transport in Dublin after 11.30, and taking a girl to the north side after a dance involved a long, lonely and solo walk home in the early morning.

One night at the Four Provinces Ballroom I met the Queen of the

After a stroll up Grafton Street one could go through the the impressive gates that led to St. Stephen's Green and relax there in the lovely gardens.

ENTRANCE TO ST. STEPHEN'S GREEN FROM GRAFTON STREET, DUBLIN. VR. 1677.

World. She had dark hair, blue eyes and teeth like pearls. When she smiled the music stopped. In the silence she threw her head back and laughed; the music started again but it was no longer the band playing; angels had descended from Heaven and were playing harps all over the place. I was dancing on air. Then I spotted the friend and, me being a very good friend, decided he should be called witness to the miracle that had befallen me.

I called him over.

I introduced him.

He asked her where she was from.

'Glasnevin.'

Then I was swept off my feet again. This time by him. He took me into a corner and asked me if I knew what I was doing. Did I know where Glasnevin was? I said I thought it was on the branch line to Heaven. He said it was four miles 'the far side of the bridge'. He was a strong friend. Not only persuasive, muscular, too. He said if I dreamed of taking her home he'd beat sense into me when I got back.

Having a terrible distaste for violence, I gave in to him. I sulked but I gave in. It was 8 March 1966. I'll never forget it. I was walking home with my friend. I was sulking. My thoughts were on the other side of the river. I was thinking where I would be now if I had had my way. I would be standing at her doorstep making plans for our future together. It was exactly two in the morning when the earth moved. Even I knew that it wasn't just the thinking about her that did it. The explosion came from the centre of the city. My friend, never one to miss an opportunity to claim influence with great powers said: 'Aren't you the lucky man you listened to me.'

Maybe I was.

The next morning it was reported that policemen on patrol on O'Connell Street had found the remains of Lord Nelson in the centre of O'Connell Street. 'Persons unknown' had blown up the stone figure who had reigned so long over the centre of Dublin that he had become known as the most famous Dubliner of them all.

And they're off! The bicycle was a very popular mode of transport in Dublin of the 50s. Young men liked drop handlebars. Young ladies thought it was very feminine to stand up on their bikes when they were taking off; this also gave them greater power for peddling.

Opposite:
Handiwork of 'persons unknown'. This stump is all that was left of Nelson's Pillar in the centre of Dublin on the morning of 8 March 1966. The IRA said they didn't do it.

CHAPTER EIGHT

'Céad Míle Fáilte!'

'*Céad míle fáilte.* It means a hundred thousand welcomes. We Irish love extremes. We are extravagant. Extravagant in drink, in words, in laughter, but we are especially extravagant with our emotions. We love to love and if we can't love then we love to scorn. We don't like mediocrity too much. One is either a saint, a devil, or not Irish at all. This extravagance manifests itself in our greeting of welcome: *Céad míle fáilte.*'

We don't give you one or two, or even ten welcomes – we give you a hundred thousand of them. A million, I suppose, would be considered ostentatious but a hundred thousand is just right for us. Extravagance without vulgarity.

We have extended the welcome so often and so well. When the Pope come to Ireland in 1979, one in three of the population was there in Phoenix Park, Dublin, to welcome him. Those who didn't live in the city came up the night before and stayed with relations and friends. People opened their doors and spare bedrooms to strangers; they gave them shelter so that they would be able to see the pontiff in the morning. Before the birds were in full song, at five and six in the morning, those who lived in Dublin and those who had billeted there overnight for the occasion started walking to Phoenix Park. On the way everyone talked saying how wonderful it was and what a great man he was and how welcome he was. We'd show the world the welcome we could extend.

Céad míle fáilte.

It was genuine. People felt it.

When JFK came in June 1963 everyone in the country wanted to see him. Yes – everyone – and that is no Irish exaggeration. I remember it well. Nobody talked about anything else. The country came to halt. Television was still fairly new in 1963 but the camera crews of the world came to witness the welcome the President, a lost son of Ireland, was going to get. The Kennedy home down in Dunganstown, County Wexford, is very remote. To this day you cannot drive a car out on that road from New Ross without extreme caution. You have constantly to be listening for tractors. If you hear one coming, you have to back up to a gateway to allow it to pass. There are parts of that road where you have to back up a quarter of a mile to find a spot that will allow the passing. It doesn't happen that often because there isn't a whole lot of traffic on that road at any time. You can imagine the problem the Cadillacs and Chevrolets that the Kennedy

One in three of the population was in Dublin's Phoenix Park to welcome the Pope on his visit to Ireland in 1979. The man on the pope's right is Bishop Eamon Casey.

The woman with her eye on the cake is Mary Ryan, JFK's 62-year-old cousin. Her daughter Mary Ann holds the plate in one hand and a pot of tea in the other. Mary Ryan is now dead; Mary Ann still lives in Dunganstown and she keeps the cup the President drank out of in a glass case beside the fire where he sat when he visited them.

OPPOSITE:
Her Serene Highness Princess Grace of Monaco on a visit to Ireland. Her grandfather was a Kelly from Mayo.

PP236–7:
The Kennedy motorcade.

entourage would have in getting to the place where he was to meet his ancestors. It was 'no go'. They had to leave the big cars in the town and take Jeeps and Land Rovers to the scene of the big welcome. Kennedy himself dropped down from the sky in a field across from the house. Usually only the rain drops down in Ireland but back in 1963 the man himself did, and appropriate enough that was too, because it was as significant to the Irish as a second coming. *Céad míle fáilte.* When Grace Kelly came to visit her ancestral home in Mayo the country came to another standstill. We couldn't do enough for her. The priests and even a bishop or two were tripping over their surpluses, soutanes and purple sashes to be first to extend the hand of welcome. Policemen and soldiers lined the way and they were as excited as the people who had come to see her. Their minds and eyes were on the fairytale princess as she motored through their midst. No danger or security risk here. They were, like the rest of us, only interested in getting a close up look at Her Royal Highness, Princess Grace of Monaco, formerly one of our own, a Kelly from Mayo.

Céad míle fáilte.

Others – less distinguished guests with no know blood connection – got the welcome, too. I remember in the fifties when Bill Haley came: the south side of Dublin was like an All-Ireland Final day in Croke Park. There were flags and banners but this time no clergy – Bill himself and his Comets were the only ones with a hint of purple here. Still, they were all welcome.

Céad míle fáilte.

Jayne Mansfield came and she got a welcome even larger than the ample bosom she had carted all the way across the Atlantic. And definitely definitely no purple here, not even a bit of black. The Bishop of Kerry spoke to the public through his priests. He told the priests what they were to say to their flocks on the visit of the Blonde Bombshell. He told them they were to tell us she was welcome as the flowers of May. Everyone's welcome to Ireland's shores. The lady was welcome but she was an Occasion of Sin. We were to be nice and friendly and wave and all, but no one was to go to see her cabaret.

Jayne Mansfield wanted to show her bosom to the boys of Ireland but the Bishop of Kerry said they shouldn't look. He said Jayne was an Occasion of Sin.

Céad míle fáilte, Jayne babe!

I was a young teacher in Dublin when an excited adolescent student came gasping in the door ten minutes late after lunch. 'I saw her, sir! I saw her!' Jean Shrimpton, the iconic sixties model, had opened a new shop in Grafton Street and this student had risked my wrath to see her. I was going to get tough but I didn't. I thawed instead and said:

Céad míle fáilte, Jean.

Dead or alive they were welcome. Sometimes more welcome dead than alive! Executed by the British in August 1916 for treason, Roger Casement came home to Dublin to a hero's welcome in 1965. Plenty of purple here, and brass, top, of course. The route to Glasnevin cemetery was lined with people who watched the Mercedes cars roll by. All the hierarchy was there: bishops, priests, brothers, nuns and a cardinal with rows of buttons down his front. We were bringing home what was left of Roger Casement after nearly fifty years in a lime-filled grave in London. I don't know how welcome he would have been if he were alive. But dead as a doornail Roger got the treatment:

Céad míle fáilte, Roger.

*

But if the welcomes were extravagant, so were the rejections. If we didn't want you we sent you into exile. And for us Irish it was not just exile; that wouldn't do at all. No, it had to be 'bitter exile'. I remember learning history in school. A sad – or, rather, 'very sad' – history it was. Every chapter recounted renewed efforts by patriots to drive the occupiers from the land and every chapter ended in 'bitter' defeat. The teacher and the writer of the history books seemed to be satisfied enough with the conclusion of these events. They didn't complain about our misfortune or lack of success in objective achievement. Rather, they capitalized on it. The inevitable end to every episode was an announcement of defeat: 'though they fought bravely victory was not to be theirs'. And if the patriots were not captured and tortured in the Tower of London they went into exile.

Exile and/or martyrdom seemed as much an end as victory.

This is the flip side to this *céad míle fáilte* coin – if you are not welcomed you must be rejected. It was a mark of distinction to be exiled. If one didn't succeed in getting the *céad míle fáilte*, the best alternative

The distinguished looking man with the beard is Sir Roger Casement. This picture was taken on Tory Island. Roger was executed for treason in London in 1916 and buried there in a lime filled grave. Nearly fifty years later, in 1965, his remains were brought home and re-interred in Glasnevin Cemetery, Dublin.

was a 'bitter exile'. There was no point in living out a normal uneventful life as a non-achiever. If you weren't successful and *céad míle fáilte*-ed, then a respectable alternative was exile. If you couldn't be officially rejected there was only one thing for it and that was to induce exile.

Sean O'Casey, already mentioned in the previous chapter, was born of a Protestant family in Dublin. He was one of thirteen children. Only five survived past infancy. His father died when Sean was three years old. He had little chance of schooling and taught himself to read at the age of fourteen. Active in the Trade Union movement he also played some small part in the Easter Rising 1916, for which he was arrested. He was released without trial.

O'Casey went on to write plays about war and revolution, Irish ones at first. He cast a light of imperfection on 'patriotism'. He focused on the tragedy of death and loss. The women were the characters who suffered the detrimental effects of the actions of the would-be heroes. In *Juno and the Paycock* Johnny Boyle echoes the sentiment of the young revolutionary with the words: 'Ireland only

Sean O'Casey's eyes were dim but he had sharp insight into the depths of human tragedy. In his plays it was not the actions of would be patriot-heroes that was highlighted but the detrimental impact these actions had on the stronger background characters – wives, mothers and sweethearts. The man with him in this picture is the director, Sam Wannamaker.

half-free will never be at peace while she has a son left to pull a trigger.' But it is his mother, Mrs Boyle, who rings the bell of truth with her lament after he is dead; she says, 'He wasn't a Diehard or a Stater, but only a poor dead son.'

People accepted *Juno*. It showed a new side to revolutionary movements. It moved sympathy away from the hero to the ones who suffer the consequence of his actions. *The Plough and the Stars* went further. It pictured the men who were supposed to be doing the fighting as drunken dreamers and big talkers who achieved little. This was too much for the audiences. It undermined Irish patriotism, and that did it. Riots broke out at the Abbey in 1926 when his play was performed there. The Irish wouldn't have such a portrayal of Irish Patriotism. Still, O'Casey wasn't exiled. The Abbey did reject his next play and then O'Casey chose exile for himself. At the age of forty-six, and nearly blind, he went into voluntary exile and refused permission for his plays to be performed in Ireland.

The original Abbey Theatre in Dublin, as well known for performances from audience as from actors. There could be riots if patriotism or Catholicism were shown in a poor light.

In a biography of O'Casey, Atkinson says: 'First time in his life, Sean felt a surge of hatred for Cathleen ni Houlihan sweeping over him. He saw now that the one who had the walk of a queen could be a bitch at times. She galled the hearts of her children who dared to be above the ordinary, and she often slew the best ones. She had hounded Parnell to death, she had yelled and torn at Yeats, at Synge, and now she was doing the same to him. What an old snarly gob she could be at times; an ignorant one too.'

My own interpretation of O'Casey's choice is that he couldn't get the *céad míle fáilte*, so he took a respectable alternative: he took his ball and went home.

James Joyce (1882–1941) was born two years after O'Casey, and he also took his genius to flourish in other grounds. His reasons and circumstances were altogether different. Joyce was born into a wealthy family. The Joyces didn't stay wealthy, but that was not because of any tragedy, rather because James' father was a spendthrift and

James Joyce (1882-1941) was an intellectual, a linguist and an Irish Catholic but he cared neither for religion nor for patriotism.

dreamer. He was at a distance from reality similar to the characters in O'Casey's plays. It wasn't patriotism but romanticism of another form that was his nemesis. Joyce, too, was uninfluenced by love of country or religion. He was a true intellectual and a linguist. He was an academic achiever, and, apart from having no interest in what was commonly know as 'the Cause', he thought nationalism and religion were divisive factors unworthy of any respect. He took off to the Continent because he liked language and because he felt stifled in Catholic Ireland. His mother took ill and Joyce returned home in 1902. He refused to kneel in prayer at her bedside and when that did not get him exiled he went off anyway. He took Nora Barnacle with him and lived 'in sin' with her for thirty years before he married her. He did make two return trips, the first in 1909 to open a cinema (the Volta Picture Palace), and again in 1912 in an effort to have *Dubliners* published. Dublin refused and Joyce never returned. He said he felt disowned by Ireland. He must have kept an accurate picture of the place in mind because, although *Ulysses* records Dublin in great detail, Joyce wrote it all 'in exile'.

You'd nearly think Samuel Beckett (1906–89) himself chose the day to be born. Not only was it Friday the 13th, it was a Good Friday as well. Appropriate, indeed, for a man who claimed to be incapable of joy and happiness. He said he was consistent only in his loneliness.

The morose Samuel Beckett (1906-89) said he got no joy from life. He seemed to be sorrowfully resistant to everything, including the advances from the daughter of James Joyce.

Beckett left Ireland for Paris at the age of twenty-two and met up with fellow exile Joyce there. He was greatly influenced by him. He visited Joyce regularly but it is reported that, as in his later plays, nothing really happened during their meetings. Oftentimes no words were spoken. They just wallowed in each other's loneliness and unhappiness. I would like to think it was because they missed their native shore, that they were praying for a welcome home, a *céad míle fáilte*, but I am afraid it was not so. Both were willing exiles.

Though women could not resist him, Beckett resisted all their overtures, or mostly. By way of explanation for turning down James Joyce's daughter's advances, he said he was dead and had no feelings that were human. Still, I think he must have had been secretly addicted to the *céad míle fáilte*, or, that failing, the alternative – exile. Having voluntarily taken himself out of Ireland he went on to have himself ejected from Paris. He had joined the French Resistance movement there, as a consequence of which he had to leave the occupied zone. He could not return until after the war.

Even Brendan Behan dallied with exile. True to character, he tried it

TOP: Brendan Behan, as well known for drinking as he was for writing, boarding a plane for Dublin after being charged with drunkenness in 1959. ABOVE: Stealing scene and cigar from Harpo Marx.

in some unorthodox ways. After serving time as a 'guest of Her Majesty' in London he had himself exiled from Britain. For most of his life he was *persona non grata* there. He was, in fact, forbidden entry. However, since it was possible to go to England without a passport, Behan was often able to breach his lack of welcome over there. He also went to Paris. He wouldn't have been moving in the same circles as Beckett and Joyce. He went as a house painter. Even if he had been sitting at a boulevard café he wouldn't have had much time for the long silences of the other two men, and he certainly wouldn't have been sipping coffee. Behan was a drinking, shouting man. When he did meet with success and acclaim, where did he achieve it? In Ireland of the welcome? No chance! The same Britain that had exiled him finally clasped him to her bosom. Perhaps that is a hyperbolic assessment of what really was a ridiculing of the 'drunken Paddy'. He was assured notoriety, if not fame, after appearing on Malcolm Muggeridge's TV show. He was so drunk he was hardly able to talk. Live on screen, he spat out extravagant claims to greatness. Ireland, having refused him the fame he so thirstily sought, he portrayed himself as the exiled son who had to go overseas to have his genius recognized.

Innovative use of the wellie boot

Returning Americans – Irish Americans coming home – were awful welcome. You couldn't believe how welcome. All the family would be down at the boat, or, later, up at the airport to meet them. Ironically, as the Americans started returning, in the fifties, the outward flow had still not been stemmed. Those going out and the returning ones were passing themselves out with suitcases on gangways and railway platforms. The returning Yank was something close to a miracle.

I remember the coming home of one of my uncles from America. We had a lot of aunts and uncles over there. Not all kept in touch but Paddy (that was his name – not to be confused with Den Paaty of an earlier chapter, an uncle of my mother's) did. He was working in Boston and he had a Chevrolet. He sent home pictures of it and him. He had a band. He sent home a ticket of admittance to one of the functions his band had played at. It said 'Music by Paddy Duggan and his Orchestra'. That to me proved he was extraordinary and famous. The ticket was kept in a jug on the dresser of my granny's house. Anyone who came in was shown the proof of stardom in the family. Now he was coming home.

There was a problem. We lived about sixty miles from my granny's house and, until we got the car in 1949, had to take the train. We thought the man with the band might send the fare for all of us to come and see him. He didn't; I am sure he never thought of it; he would have forgotten how hard it was to raise that kind of money. Anyway, we waited until a few days before he was to go back and then my mother decided there was nothing for it but to go and see him. She had only the fare for herself and one of us. I was the chosen one. I was obedient and would stay quiet and not shame her in front of the Yank.

I will never forget him. He had nearly white trousers, a pink shirt and suede shoes. He spoke with an American accent; he said he had an apartment, that steak was a pound a pound but that he still bought it. I was aghast at such wealth. But to confirm his status as a real Yank he said he

The beautiful Maureen O'Hara and The Duke on the set of The Quiet Man *during the making of the film in Mayo. The lovely lady is now in her eighties, still speaks with a brogue and comes home to Ireland twice a year.*

liked it with a few 'to-may-toes'. To me he was not just from across the Atlantic: I thought he must have come from somewhere near Heaven. He gave me a dollar for myself and one each for my brother and sisters.

Céad míle fáilte, Uncle Paddy.

He returned the next day. Before he did, he thanked us all for the welcome we gave him. He said it was wonderful the way Irish people welcomed home the Yanks.

One of the reason Paddy would have gone to America was to make room at home for his younger brother to marry and bring in a wife. That was one of the problems with the farming community. Only one boy could inherit the land, the others had to get out of the way. Meeting a partner was a problem. It wasn't so much lack of venues, but it was difficult to find someone suitable. The chosen one had not only to suit the partner; she or he had to satisfy other conditions, too.

There were matchmakers. They kept their eyes and ears open. They knew everyone around and they knew a lot about them. Fathers and mothers would consult them to see if they had anyone suitable for their son and daughter. If they had them, the parents of the two involved were brought together to hammer out a deal. The amount of land the boy had, or was heir to, was weighed against the dowry the girl's parents could raise for her. The dowry was mostly to pay off the other brothers and sisters who would be expected to leave the home to make room for the new woman.

The welcome that was extended to these girls marrying into the family was in some proportion to the amount they brought with them. The 'marrying in' girl could be very stiff if she had a good dowry. She might be the one who had the upper hand, if she had a good dowry. The tables could easily be turned on the people of the house. If part of the deal for the marriage was that the son inherit the farm before the marriage, she might be the one the older folk were then beholden to for the *céad míle fáilte*.

Not long ago, a young man I know – Seamus – told me he had a problem. He said he wanted to marry this very nice girl he had met. He had proposed to her and she had said she wanted to marry him but that she was doubtful because he lived with his father and she would have to move into the house with the two of them. The boy's mother was dead.

The Irish are great believers in good conversation; they always were. The women (above) are taking a break from working with turf while those below talk over the fish they are trying to sell.

OPPOSITE:
Any sporting event brought people out. (above) Victorious currach rowers shouldered by supporters in Galway, and nobody is taking any chances with the sun at a GAA match (below) between Waterford and Galway in Ennis, Co. Clare in 1938.

'I take my hat off to you.'
People often say this if they
admire something that is
done. It seems the man in
this picture at a hurling
semi-final between Tipperary
and Galway believes action
speaks louder than words.

Opposite:
(above) Fishmonger in
Dublin's Moore Street.
(below) Skirts on their way
up and hair on its way
down indicate that this
picture of women in
O'Connell Street, Dublin
was taken in the 60s.

I asked him what her reservations were; the boy and his father lived in a very fine house with all modern conveniences. He said she would feel insecure. She said the place was still belonging to his father and she would feel like a servant girl to the two of them. She wanted him to get his father to 'sign over the place', and then she would marry him. He said he couldn't ask his father to do that. Would I do it for him?

I visited the father, Jimmy, and after a few whiskeys and a bit of chat about the weather and harvest I told him about Seamus and the girl he wanted to marry. I told him she wanted the place signed over before she would accept. Jimmy refused. He didn't say he wouldn't do it but I knew by him he didn't want to, and I was sorry I had asked. There was an awkward silence, and then he said, 'You'll think I'm mean.' I said no I wouldn't; I said it was his business, that I became involved just because I thought it a pity the son couldn't be married. I said I thought it would be nice to have a woman about the house, that it was difficult for two men to live alone. Then, Jimmy said he would tell me why he wouldn't do it.

He told me he had married a girl who had the same problem as the one Seamus wanted to marry. She didn't want to marry into the place until it was in his name. He talked to his father and his father said okay; if that was what was required that is what he would do. Anything, he said, to make the girl feel welcome into their home.

They married and she moved in. She made herself awful welcome. She also made her own family welcome. She invited them to come and stay. They did. They stayed often and they stayed long. Jimmy didn't say a word. He was awful fond of his wife, and he was a bit afraid of her, too. Seamus was born and their happiness and joy knew no bounds. Jimmy's father was as happy as Jimmy himself. Grandfather and grandson became very close. The grandfather knew what Seamus was saying even before his parents understood him; they used to walk through the fields together, gabbling away in childish gibberish – they understood each other. Jimmy's wife became a little jealous. She would take the child away from the grandfather as much as she could. However, the attachment between them was so great she wasn't too successful at that.

She began to shun the old man. Jimmy told me it hurt him to see the way 'she flung the bit of grub at him'. Still he said nothing. He couldn't. He loved his wife. A woman of very strong will, she didn't take too easily to instruction, or even suggestion. Jimmy told me that oftentimes he'd be working in the fields when he'd see his father coming towards him. He'd be all hunched up with unhappiness. He never complained, Jimmy said. But he knew his father was very hurt. He knew his wife had been keeping the child from him.

After a few years the old man became a little unsteady on his feet. He had to be helped. Jimmy was happy to help him but his wife said he couldn't afford the time. She said he should be out in the fields doing the work and not be inside the house helping the father. She said people would start talking about how foolish they were to leave the place to go to wrack and ruin minding an old man instead of looking after things.

In the end she said there was a place for old people like Jimmy's father. She said he would be happier in a place like that. She said he would be looked after and cared for and they could look after the farm in peace. Jimmy gave in to her. He agreed to 'commit' his father to the County Home.

They tackled up the horse and trap and got the father in. Seamus cried and refused to go to school. He said he wanted to go to the 'hospital' with his beloved granddad. The mother said 'No.' She said his place was in school. She said, 'Off with you now, they will make your grandfather better in 'hospital'. Jimmy told me how bad he felt. He told me it was the first time he had crossed his wife but he insisted that Seamus come with them to put the granddad into the County Home. She huffed. She threw off the coat and she said, 'Okay then, have it your own way. Take the child with you, but if you do I am not going.' She stormed into the house.

They drove the horse and trap to the place and the grandfather was signed in. Seamus was in great anguish. He was too young to understand exactly what was happening. He thought this was a place that all old people had to go to when they were sick. He was looking all around the place and crying away. Jimmy knew by the way he was looking around that he was trying to remember the place. He was a little afraid that Seamus might be planning on returning here. He said

This Aran Island man is well 'tweeded' against the winds that have sculptured his face, while his weathered hands and her own youth protect the curly haired little girl.

to his son, 'Don't be looking around like that, you can't be coming to a place like this. This place is only for old people.' 'I know that,' Seamus said. 'I am just looking around so that I will know where I have to bring you when you are old and sick.'

That opened Jimmy's eyes. He brought his father home with him. The wife wasn't too happy but she had to put up with it.

'So that is why I won't be signing the place over,' Jimmy said. 'There is no place like home,' he said, 'as long as it is your home.'

The Irish have always been famous for their welcome. They still are – the hundred thousand is not an exaggeration in many ways. If they exercise a little caution here and there about extending it, it is not perhaps without some reason.

In yesterday's Ireland there was no great strain on the Irish welcome; the incoming traffic was light. We could afford to say, indeed sing: 'The door is always open and there's a welcome on the mat.'

Other lands accepted those who had to leave Irish shores through poverty and famine. Now things have changed utterly. The traffic of poor and hungry people is no longer outward. People from other countries now seek solace on our shores.

Let's hope the Ireland of today and tomorrow continues to extend its *céad míle fáilte* to them.

A cart load of turf in Co. Sligo. Loads so small were most unusual. The animal might be a mule; he has that look about him. He might have refused to take more. They were notorious for stubbornness.

Index

Page numbers in *italic type* refer to pictures or their captions

A DAVID & CHARLES BOOK

First published in the UK in 2003

Copyright © Paddy Linehan 2003

Distributed in North America
by F&W Publications, Inc.
4700 East Galbraith Road
Cincinnati, OH 45236
1-800-289-0963

Paddy Linehan has asserted his right to be identified as author of this work in accordance with the Copyright, Designs and Patents Act, 1988.

All rights reserved. No part of this publication may be reproduced, stored in a retrieval system, or transmitted, in any form or by any means, electronic or mechanical, by photocopying, recording or otherwise, without prior permission in writing from the publisher.

A catalogue record for this book is available from the British Library.

ISBN 0 7153 1577 3

Printed in Great Britain by Butler & Tanner Ltd
for David & Charles
Brunel House   Newton Abbot   Devon

Visit our website at www.davidandcharles.co.uk

David & Charles books are available from all good bookshops; alternatively you can contact our Orderline on (0)1626 334555 or write to us at FREEPOST EX2110, David & Charles Direct, Newton Abbot, TQ12 4ZZ (no stamp required UK mainland).

Commissioning Editor: **Jane Trollope**
Project Editor: **Richard Collins**
Desk Editor: **Shona Wallis**
Art Editor: **Sue Cleave**
Production Controller: **Jennifer Campbell**

PICTURE ACKNOWLEDGEMENTS

Hulton Archive: pp 1, 2,4, 22, 30, 32, 35(btm), 38, 42, 44, 45(btm), 57, 74, 77, 87, 93, 101, 125, 144, 146, 149, 151, 157, 159, 160, 163, 165, 170, 176, 182, 183, 185, 206, 207, 214, 216, 222, 224, 238, 240, 245(top), 250
Corbis: 6, 21, 117, 178, 181, 186, 208, 212, 236, 239, 242, 243, 244(top), 245(btm)
Bord Fáilte: 8, 10, 12, 13, 14, 19, 26, 27, 29, 31, 34, 35(top), 40, 41, 48, 51, 53, 55, 60, 61, 62, 64, 67, 68, 70, 80, 81, 82, 83, 85(inset), 86, 89, 90, 94, 96, 97, 100, 102, 105, 108, 133, 138, 154, 156, 194, 197, 204, 210(btm), 211, 221, 225, 230, 232, 248, 249(top), 252
G.A. Duncan: 11, 56, 58, 63, 76, 88, 91, 98, 114, 192, 198, 200, 213, 218, 247
National Library of Ireland: 15, 24, 25, 33(top), 111, 118, 130, 132, 135, 136, 152, 169, 175, 196, 210(top), 219, 223, 226, 227, 228, 229, 232, 241, 251, 253
Cork Examiner: 16, 17, 36, 37, 45(top), 46, 47, 50, 54, 65, 66, 73, 78, 84(main), 92, 95, 103, 107, 113, 116, 124, 128, 134, 143, 172, 174, 179, 187, 191, 199, 202, 220, 249(btm)
Tom Graves: 18, 28, 52, 110, 112, 120, 121, 131, 141, 188, 234
Seamus Healey: 20, 33(btm), 43, 71, 201, 215, 246
Jim & Marguerite Byrne: 59, 119, 122, 126